About the Author

The author, an attorney, advocate, administrator, and rabbi, lives in Jerusalem, the center of the universe.

The Beach Boy Volume II, Aliyah

William Semenow

The Beach Boy Volume II, Aliyah

Olympia Publishers
London

www.olympiapublishers.com
OLYMPIA PAPERBACK EDITION

Copyright © William Semenow 2024

The right of William Semenow to be identified as author of this work has been asserted in accordance with sections 77 and 78 of the Copyright, Designs and Patents Act 1988.

All Rights Reserved

No reproduction, copy or transmission of this publication may be made without written permission. No paragraph of this publication may be reproduced, copied or transmitted save with the written permission of the publisher, or in accordance with the provisions of the Copyright Act 1956 (as amended).

Any person who commits any unauthorized act in relation to this publication may be liable to criminal prosecution and civil claims for damage.

A CIP catalogue record for this title is available from the British Library.

ISBN: 978-1-80439-933-0

While this book is based on the author's life, names of many of the characters in it are fictional as are some of the incidents and characters therein. Any resemblance to actual persons, living or dead, is purely coincidental.

First Published in 2024

Olympia Publishers
Tallis House
2 Tallis Street
London
EC4Y 0AB

Printed in Great Britain

Dedication

I dedicate this book to my wife, my children and grandchildren, and my siblings and their families who all played an important role in helping me along the writing process. Special thanks to our Cleveland "family" without whom I never would be who I am today.

Acknowledgments

Many thanks to my wife, who encouraged me to write this memoir and allowed me the time and space to do so. Special thanks to my daughter and son-in-law in the U.K. and to my dear friend and family member, Mr. Larry Levine of London and to Mrs. Helena Stern of Jerusalem, all of whom read the manuscript and offered insightful comments and corrections.

CHAPTER I
Aliyah

Our bleary eyed and increasingly irritable family of five stumbled onto the Holy Land at six in the morning, after an eleven hour El Al Flight from New York, on 17 July 1986, with thirteen suitcases and trunks. Our lift preceded us.

We had made *Aliyah*—the Hebrew word which literally means "to go up" or "to be elevated." Our immigration to Israel, our *Aliyah,* was meant to be an elevation in a spiritual sense. I was hoping to feel an electric shock or tremor as my feet hit the ground, but I did not. Holiness is not only geographical. It requires preparation and the concentration of a clear mind. Mine was anything but. And we first had to deal with *Aliyah's* more mundane aspects.

On that morning in Ben Gurion Airport, near Tel Aviv, we had our first physical encounter with official Israeli bureaucracy. In making *Aliyah* from America, everything had been done through the Cleveland *Aliyah* representative and the Israeli consulate in Chicago. Everyone there, in the "Old Country," was smiling, encouraging, solicitous and friendly. They made us feel that we were doing Israel a great favor by deigning to move from our privileged first world country to a desert populated with tents, camels, Bedouins, and Jewish pioneers. That was a façade. Now that we were on Israeli soil, there was no more "Mr. Israeli Nice Guy." It was—"Meet Bureaucracy

Israeli Style." They quickly let us know that they were doing us a favor to let us settle in their Land.

We, together with the other immigrants, were herded into a large and almost empty hall furnished with folding wooden picnic tables and plastic chairs. We waited our turn to approach a table at which a young woman immigration officer was seated.

As new documents, like passports, identity cards, and benefit booklets, were to be issued, the first order of business was spelling our names in Hebrew. We were allowed to officially change our first names to our Hebrew ones. (When I was born, Jews in the diaspora were usually given two sets of names at birth—Hebrew ones, which were not officially registered on our birth certificates, and *goyishe* (non-Jewish) ones which were. My wife and I did so. Our children's legal names were already Hebrew ones.

She asked me how I spelled my last name. I told her "s*amech mem nun vuv vais*—'Semonow.'" (The "w" at the end of a Russian name is pronounced as "v").

She told me matter-of-factly, "You can't spell your last name that way."

"But that's how it's spelled," I said. "It's how my ancestors spelled it. It's spelled that way in our *kesubah* (marriage contract) and on all Hebrew documents I ever signed."

"Sorry, but you can't spell it that way. You must spell it: *samech yud mem vav nun vuv;* or *samech yud mem nun vuv.*"

"But that spells 'Simono' or 'Simonov.' That's not my name. It's 'Semonov.'"

"Sorry, we can't spell it the way you want. Pick one of the two choices I gave you," she said in a polite but resolute voice.

We had just endured an eleven-hour flight and it was now

seven in the morning. Miriam, our eight-year-old, Rochi, our four-year-old and baby Binyamin hadn't slept on the plane, and I could see that if I didn't give in, I would be stuck in Immigration Purgatory with my family—three screaming young children—for who knows how long.

I rationalized to myself. "Semonow" anyway wasn't our real name. When the government in nineteenth century Eastern Europe made us take last names, my progenitor, whose father's name was probably "Shimon," Russified it to "Semenow." At the time, our *shtetl* in Lithuania was ruled by the Russians, but the Jewish Pale of Settlement of Eastern Europe kept seesawing back and forth between Russia and Poland. With changes in government came changes in surname. It was either *Semenow* or *Semenovich,* depending on who our ruler was. We had *Senat* relatives in South Africa and *Semenovich* cousins in the States. I told myself that it didn't really matter that much. I chose *samech yud mem vav nun vuv*—"Simonov."

Although I didn't know it at the time, I could then have claimed the Hebrew moniker *"freir."* It's a borrowed Yiddish word like many words and expressions in Hebrew. *Freir* is a derivative of the German *"frei"* or free. It means an easy mark, a simpleton, a sucker—someone who is easily taken advantage of. Because I had been brought up in polite society, I almost never raise my voice. I make it a point never to argue too much with unreasonable people. And I could tell that Miss Immigration Officer was unreasonable. My mistake. A *freir* is the last thing an Israeli wants to be. Once you are marked as a *freir* you're the butt of every other joke and fair game for all.

An Israeli in my position would have screamed back at that young Jewish girl clerk, "What do you take me for, little girl? A fool? Don't give me that idiotic routine about how you can't spell my name the way it's been spelled for generations. I'm not buying it. I know you can do it and if you don't want to, I demand to speak to your boss! And if he or she doesn't agree I'm going to call my cousin Shimon Peres. You've heard his name? He's the Prime Minister! And he's my first cousin once removed and my grandfather's *landsman* from Minsk. I hope you liked working here, because after today all you'll have left are your memories. Now I'm not moving and not signing anything until you spell my name correctly! The way I tell you to!"

But, as I said, I wasn't an Israeli yet. I've been here in Israel for thirty-five years now and I'm still not Israeli. I couldn't give her the dressing down that she deserved. I am still a *freir*.

Having finished the immigration paperwork, we were assigned a government driver who loaded his van with our luggage and drove us to our friends' house in the Ramot neighborhood of Jerusalem—the Weissmans. They had offered to let us stay with them until we could move into the apartment, we were renting in nearby Maalot Dafna. Our furniture was in a lift on a Zim line cargo ship making its slow way from New York to Haifa via the Pacific Islands and China, or so it seemed.

To encourage our immigration, the Israeli government allowed us a greatly subsidized and duty-free lift. A lift is a ship container that measures 8ft (2.43m) wide, 8.5ft (2.59m) high and 20ft (6.06m) in length. It sat in our driveway in Cleveland for a week and we filled it up with everything in our house, except for my baby grand piano, and a decrepit and out of tune upright, which was ready for the piano cemetery, and the kitchen sink. As for the baby grand, the small Israeli apartment we were renting wouldn't have accommodated both it and our dining room table. The table was more important. Instead, I purchased a more practical electronic piano. And, I was told, the apartment came with a kitchen sink.

After packing the lift, we still had enough room left over that I could have put my Mazda sports car in it, but as Mazda wasn't being sold in Israel at that time, I wouldn't be able to get it serviced. And I was no mechanic. I sold it together with our Volvo station wagon.

CHAPTER II
Background to the Decision

Aliyah was not just about moving to another country and making a fresh start. It was not just the fulfillment of the dreams of my ancestors and the inheritance of my Homeland. It was not a decision born only from a spiritual quest, but it was also motivated by very personal reasons.

I'm a *baal teshuva*—a returnee to classical Judaism. I didn't have a religious education, aside from the very meager smattering of knowledge taught to us in Hebrew School for six hours a week up to my Bar Mitzvah at thirteen. The sum of what I remember learning in Hebrew School are three words and their translation: הוא, pronounced: *"who,"* is "he" in English; היא *"he"* is "she"; and a דג *"dog"* is a "fish." It's entirely possible that I learnt some other words in Hebrew, but those anomalous ones are the ones that stuck. After becoming religious I started to learn more, but never enough to feel that I was on par with my friends who had been brought up in religious homes and schools.

Like many others in my generation, I was born into a family of proud, but not particularly religious Jews. My father, *alov hashalom (a"h*—may he rest in peace) was from Mt. Pleasant, a small town in Westmoreland County in Western Pennsylvania, about forty miles from Pittsburgh. His parents were both *Likvaks*—from *shtetlach* (small villages) in a part of Lithuania, which was then ruled by Poland. My mother was from the Bronx. Her father was from Bialystock, also in Lithuania, and her mother, from Bucharest, Romania. All my grandparents came to the U.S. between 1894 and 1906.

From the time that millions of Jews from Eastern Europe began pouring into the United States—the late 1880s to the 1920s—there had been a steep decline in *halachic* (ritual) observance. Many factors were involved, but that's for another book. By the start of the Second World War, Orthodox Judaism in America was all but dead. Because of the relative absence of overt anti-Semitism, coupled with opportunities for higher education, unavailable to most Jews in the Old Country, Jews willingly discarded their religious identities, many changed their names, and almost all tried to blend in to the wider *goyishe* society. That meant Christmas trees and Easter Eggs, in addition to *latkes* (potato pancakes) and a *menorah* on *Chanukah* and a Passover *Seder*.

Arriving on Freedom's shores after the Second World War, and seeing a religious wasteland, penniless immigrant survivors of the Holocaust, including about 10,000 Hungarian Jews (most of whom were *Chassidim*) and a few rabbis and their *talmidim* (students) from Lithuanian Yeshivos, dreamed, what seemed to many to be an impossible and quixotic dream—to revive *halachic* Judaism in America.

When I was growing up in the 1950s and early 60s, my image of a religious Jew was a *Chassid* with a filthy black caftan, long *payos (*side curls*),* and reeking of the kosher salami sandwich stuffed into his pocket. The Main Branch of the New York Public Library at Fifth Avenue and 42nd St. was his luncheonette. In those days, before the proliferation of kosher restaurants, the library offered a warm and free location for a winter's lunch break to those Jews working in the nearby Diamond District on 47th St. I never witnessed that scene, but my mother, who as a college student in the late 40's used to study in the library, described it in such vivid terms that it was as if I saw and smelled those *Chassidim* myself. I equated those salami-smelling *Chassidim* with all the religious Jews I didn't know.

The birth of the State of Israel, the horrors of the Holocaust, and the Eichmann Trial, among other factors, fostered within my generation a greater awareness of our Jewishness. The Six-Day War made us into proud Jews.

As the U.S. involvement in the Vietnamese War grew throughout the 1960s, the very real fear of being drafted into the Army and dying senselessly in a South Asian rice paddy to protect a cruel, despotic, and thoroughly corrupt regime in South Vietnam, faced our college age generation. Thoughts of death and therefore of the meaning of life, haunted us. And there was also a rumor that the wildly popular and iconic folk singer, Bob Zimmerman, *alias* Bob Dylan, was studying in a *yeshiva* in Far Rockaway. All this primed my generation of Jews to listen to the message of Orthodox Judaism. *Yeshivos* for young men and seminaries for young women led by young, dynamic, and secularly educated rabbis and their wives opened their doors to cater to us.

At this point I think it would be appropriate to review my own development as an Orthodox Jew. My great grandmother (my mother's grandmother), Deena Rochel (whom I called *Nani-Nani)*, had a major influence on my young life. We lived in a three-family house in Long Beach on the South Shore of Long Island. My mother's parents lived on the ground floor, we lived on the second and *Nani-Nani* on the third.

She told me that every day there's a "lucky moment" when *Hashem* answers our prayers. She *davened* (prayed) all day to catch that lucky time. It was well known in the family that as long as *Nani-Nani* was alive, nothing bad happened to any of her children or their families. I realize now how difficult a life she must have lived. None of her children were religious, nor were her grandchildren or great-grandchildren. As far as I know she didn't complain. Of course, she wouldn't eat in any one of her children's or grandchildren's homes, because they didn't keep kosher, or if they did, she couldn't trust their standards because they weren't *shomer Shabbos* (Sabbath observant). After she died each family started to fall apart or was stricken by illness, divorce, and other ill tidings. While her children were superstitious and believed in her ability to intervene with G-d on our behalf, no one thought to take the mantle of prayer and *mitzvohs* upon themselves and rescue us.

She died at home in 1957 at age 89. I was nine years old. Her funeral was quite unusual. It was held in the main sanctuary of our local synagogue. Normally Jewish funerals are held in funeral homes. I probably have attended hundreds of funerals since that time, and never once in a *shul*, except for funerals for *Roshei HaYeshiva* (Heads of Yeshivos), which are often held in the main *Beis Medrash* (study hall) of their *yeshiva*. Rabbi Goldberg remarked that because she was such an extraordinary woman, the *shul* wanted to honor her by making the funeral there. There were rows of rabbis in flowing caftans and broad brimmed black hats from Brooklyn who had made the hour's journey to Long Beach to pay homage to a woman who had generously supported their Jewish institutions with the meager amounts of money she had. But they didn't come because she was a donor. They came because she was a *tzaddekas*—a saintly woman—unique and outstanding in her generation.

She sang Yiddish songs to me. One that she sang repeatedly was *"Nani Nani feigaleh."* That's why I called her *Nani-Nani*. I didn't understand most of the song, but one line in the song stuck with me—*Torah iz die beste sechora*—"Torah is the best merchandise" in the world. She and that song had a profound effect on my soul. I never had a question about the existence of G-d or that Torah was Divine. It was a given.

Of course, belief in G-d is one thing, feeling obligated to do the *mitzvohs* is another. Growing up I never had the feeling that I was doing anything wrong by not keeping *Shabbos* or *kashrus*. I knew Jews who did keep them, even my best friend did. I thought that doing so was quaint and respectable. That was the tradition in their families. I liked the idea of tradition. Ours included listening to *Kiddush* that Cantor Caplow made for *Nani-Nani* in her apartment every Friday night; going to *shul* on *Rosh Hashanah* and *Yom Kippur*; having a Passover *Seder* and lighting *Chanukah* candles. These were our traditions. I never felt a need to do more.

CHAPTER III
Medical School

As my college years were ending and with the all too real prospect of being drafted into the Army and being sent to the killing fields of Vietnam, staring me in the face, I made a momentous decision.

The year before I graduated, Ritchie, one of my roommates, had applied to and was accepted by the University of Barcelona Medical School. We were all aware of three main deferments for the draft—teaching, the ministry and medical school. There were also the medical or psychological deferments of 4F or 1Y. A 4F deferment was permanent; a 1Y could get you a six-month deferment. One of my roommates, Joe Beauregard, had starved himself until he weighed less than 105 pounds, the minimum weight for a recruit of his height. He looked like the pictures I had seen of concentration camp inmates. He got a 4F. That drastic course of action was extremely dangerous and beyond my ability to replicate.

I had a history of kidney stones, and my parents sent me to William Kuntsler, a famous New York lawyer and anti-war activist, who helped young men avoid the draft legally. His office was building up a file for me as a 4F in case I needed it. But I didn't relish the thought of having to go to an induction center with my medical file in case they didn't agree with my lawyer's evaluation.

From what I heard, there were no public-school teaching

jobs available in the United States. They had all been taken by those who had graduated in preceding years. At the time, I thought becoming a minister meant a Catholic priest or a Protestant minister. I never considered that I could become a rabbi and never knew that 50 miles away in Brooklyn there existed "draft-dodging" *yeshivos,* where one could be enrolled and get a deferment and would never have to attend. But medical school sounded good, particularly since the admission standards at the University of Barcelona were lower than medical schools in the States. And the fact that it was in Spain made it sound like an adventure. I applied along with a couple of my roommates, and we were accepted.

During the whole first year of Medical School, I attended exactly one class. That was on the first day of the first semester. It was a promise I made to my mother. Her thinking was that if I'd liked that class I would go back for more and eventually become a doctor. At the time I had no intention to pursue that profession. I cringe at the sight of blood.

The University of Barcelona, in the city center, is housed in a huge, multi-story building with a red-tiled roof. Construction began in 1863. Its style of architecture has been called neo-Romanesque and is typical of municipal buildings from that period found in Spain and South America. It's a combination of early Italian Renaissance and Catalan medieval architecture. Columns and arches and marbled patios surround the inner courtyard; and wide marble staircases, stained glass windows, and large amphitheater lecture halls dominate the interior. It looked like it was straight out of a movie set for films featuring English and European universities. In fact, I was half expecting Professor Frankenstein to walk into the hall and up to the lectern.

The class I chose to attend was called "Histology." I took a seat in the middle of the hall of about seven rows above the lectern. I looked around the room. I felt out of place. The male students were mostly neatly dressed boys from upper middle-class homes and, I imagined, none were Jewish. It seemed that I had nothing in common with them. There was one girl in the class. The student sitting next to me told me that she was from Puerto Rico and had failed the first-year exams for the past seven years in a row, but she was back again. That was an amazing feature of the University. If you flunked your exams, you were entitled to repeat the year as many times as you pleased.

The professor, who was named Pujol, Casals or some other Catalan name, not remotely related to Frankenstein, entered, and stood at the lectern and began. The class, which covered background to the subject, was high school level Chemistry. After a minute, I was bored and uncomfortable. That really wasn't very surprising. After all, the Spanish students, who were ninety-nine percent of the class, were only high school graduates. In Europe, like in most of the world, students enter professional schools from high school. They don't spend four years getting an undergraduate degree. I had already taken Biology, Chemistry and Physics in college. I imagined that the rest of the courses would be as basic and boring as this. I kept my promise to my mother and now I was finished. The only time I went back to the school was to re-register for the first-year course for the subsequent two years. The truth is that even had I wanted to go to classes, I wouldn't have been able to. The school was closed for most of the time I was in Spain because of student riots and protests. But they did have exams. The serious students read the materials and took the tests. After my experience, I was always wary of Spanish doctors. How could they be trusted to know anything if a large part of their education was self-taught? In any case, the draft board accepted the letter from the University saying that I was enrolled in Medical School. It didn't say what year I was in.

During that first year in Spain, I devoted my time to photography. I had long been interested in that art form. Although I loved to draw, I wasn't very good at it. Photography offered an alternative. I got my first camera when I was about ten years old – a Kodak Brownie. It was a very simple camera and the pictures it took weren't very good. One couldn't focus the camera, so the images weren't sharp. It was fun but also expensive and you had to wait a week to ten days for the developed pictures to come back from the drug store. In Junior High, in Shop class, we learnt how to develop film. It wasn't that difficult after you practiced a few times, but I didn't have a darkroom at home and no real place to make one.

My parents bought me a 35-millimeter camera for my *bar mitzvah*. It wasn't a fancy one, but I could focus it and change the settings depending on my light meter readings. I loved it and snapped away as often as I could. My parents paid for the developing, so I wasn't careful to make sure every shot was a masterpiece. In fact, very few were decent, but gradually their quality improved. When I graduated from college, my parents bought me a Nikkormat – the cheaper Nikon. It was a very sturdy camera and the only real difference between it and the Nikon F (which was the preferred camera for professional photographers outside the studio) was that the F had a better built-in light meter. Since I had gotten used to using a handheld light meter that difference didn't matter to me at all. Both models used the same interchangeable lenses, so the quality of the images was the same. Of course, the better the lens the more expensive it was. But good used lenses were available. Although, to be honest, I always felt a little inferior with the Nikkormat body.

My friends and I lived at the Pension Central, a very dumpy rooming house off the Plaza Catalunya and next to Las Ramblas. There I met a Scot named Brian. He was a professional fashion photographer, in town for a few months for several photo-shoots. (He owned several cameras; one was, of course, a Nikon F). At first, I couldn't understand his Highland accent, but gradually I did. He lent me his different lenses, critiqued my pictures, and taught me several very valuable lessons.

The first was that the most important thing for a photographer was a good eye for a photograph. "Ye could have the best camera in the world, but if ye haven't got an eye for a good photo, it won't do ye any good."

The second was that he thought I had a good eye for pictures.

The third was to always compose the picture in the camera. One shouldn't rely on cropping the image afterwards. Each frame had to be perfectly composed.

The fourth was how to set up a darkroom, what black and white film to use and how to alter the instructions on the boxes of chemicals to get a much finer grain. He was as meticulous as a scientist and had experimented with different concentrations and temperatures of chemicals and found the perfect formula. He shared it with me. Eventually I rented my own apartment and set up my darkroom. I became a professional photographer, which didn't pay the rent. I also became an English professor, which did.

CHAPTER IV
How I Met My Wife

I was in Spain for almost three years. During my second year I met my future wife. Before I had a chance to tell her anything about myself, she told me she was Jewish. We were sitting in a restaurant, and I almost fell off my chair. What were the chances that a young, gorgeous Spanish girl was Jewish? I told her that I was also Jewish. What a coincidence! I knew that there was a small Moroccan Jewish community in Barcelona, but she told me her family was not Moroccan. They had been in Spain forever. So how was she Jewish? Her mother, whose maiden name was Duran, was from Mallorca and two summers before, while visiting her mother's family there, her uncle, her mother's brother, had shown her an old family tree, written on parchment, which had been in the family for hundreds of years. In the thirteenth and fourteenth centuries names like Rabbi Shimon Duran, Rabbi Tzemach Duran and many other rabbis appeared. Unbeknownst to the family, they were descendants of some of the greatest rabbis of the age of the *Rishonim* (great rabbis from the tenth century to the early sixteenth century).

But unlike her illustrious ancestors who fled to Algeria, her mother's branch of the family stayed in Mallorca during the various Inquisitions and converted to Christianity. Upon discovering her ancestry, Anna Maria had decided that she was Jewish.

Of course, *halachically,* there were questions. Over the

centuries there were intermarriages with non-Jewish families, so Anna probably wasn't Jewish. But she felt Jewish. Her quest to discover her Jewish roots led to the rediscovery of my own. While she was going through the process of conversion, I read all the same books. We traveled that path together.

We were married in a civil ceremony in Spain and soon after we moved to Rockville Centre, Long Island, where my family had lived since I was ten years old. The Vietnam War was winding down and I was no longer in danger of being drafted.

Our first order of business was my wife's conversion. My family wasn't religious and belonged at that time to Central Synagogue, part of the Reform movement. They had joined when my sister was old enough to go to Sunday school. The Conservative *shul* in town, which we belonged to when I was young, had a Hebrew school with classes three times a week—from 4 p.m. to 6 p.m. and three hours on Sunday mornings. My parents wanted my sister to be free for ballet and other culture enhancing classes during the week. The Reform Hebrew School was only three hours on Sunday morning.

Because of their membership, my wife did her conversion through the Central Synagogue. The rabbi was an old Polish Jew, born and raised in Warsaw before the First World War. His family had immigrated to the United States when he was a teenager and he attended Hebrew Union College in Cincinnati, where he was ordained. He also had earned a PhD in Russian Literature and, as a side job, was a professor of that subject at a local college. He oversaw conversions for the Reform Movement's Hebrew Union College in Manhattan and had supervised my wife's conversion while we were still living in Spain. The conversion course consisted of her reading about 20 books on Judaism and writing a paper on why she wanted to be Jewish. My wife got an "A" on her paper. She was now qualified to convert.

For me, the incongruity of sitting with an old Polish Jew with a strong Eastern European accent, who was also a bareheaded "rabbi", was a bit confusing. I had assumed that he had been brought up as an Orthodox Jew and had become an apostate. I was wrong. I asked him about himself and his personal beliefs. He told me that he never studied in a *yeshiva* and his parents had been Reform Jews. He was also an atheist. I almost fell off my chair. When I asked him why he was a rabbi, he said he liked the counseling aspect of the job and belief in the *Aybishter (*Yiddish for the Almighty) was not a condition for ordination at Hebrew Union College. He had only one picture in his office. It was of Albert Einstein. Einstein, apparently, was the closest thing to a divinity.

The conversion was scheduled. When I asked him about a Jewish wedding, he answered, *"dina d'malchusa dina"*—the law of the land is the law. If we had been married in a secular ceremony, he explained, he couldn't perform a Jewish one. It was a *non sequitur.* How could he perform a marriage service for people who were already married? I didn't like his answer but didn't argue with him. The conversion service consisted of the Rabbi saying *Shema Yisrael* in front of the Ark and giving my wife the name Ruth (he told us that she had no choice in the matter, that every woman convert must be renamed "Ruth"—which, as I learnt later, is false). He then gave her a certificate signed by himself and his secretary saying that Anna Maria now had the added Hebrew name of Ruth, and she was officially a Jew. Neither my wife nor I felt that this was a valid conversion ceremony. Since we had read the books he assigned, we knew that *halachically* she needed an acceptance of *mitzvohs* in front of a *Beis Din* (Jewish Court) of three observant men and *tevilah* (immersion) in a *mikveh* (a ritual bath). We also knew from our reading that the Reform movement did not believe in *halacha*.

The next Shabbos we started attending my old Conservative *shul*, Temple Beth Shalom. As the youngest married attendees, we quickly made friends with the young rabbi and his wife. I remembered Rabbi Hillel Hyman from my attendance at the synagogue before my *bar mitzvah*. In those days he was a student at JTS, the Jewish Theological Seminary in New York – the Conservative movement's rabbinical training academy and he had a job reading the Torah at Beth Shalom on *Shabbos*. He had a flair for dramatic reading that made the stories in the Torah come alive. When Rabbi Max Routtenberg retired in 1972, the Board of the *shul* voted for Rabbi Hyman as his replacement. By that time, Hillel had been appointed an Assistant Professor of Talmud at JTS.

At the same time, we met another young couple, about seven or eight years older than us, both lawyers, who were *baalei teshuva*. They were both from Rockville Centre and had gone to Southside High School, my *alma mater*. They lived in a one-bedroom apartment near the synagogue and had several small children. They were the NCSY leaders in Nassau County. NCSY, or National Council of Synagogue Youth, is a division of the Orthodox Union. The OU's symbol, found on thousands of food products, allows Jews who keep kosher to find kosher food at almost any supermarket in America.

As NCSY leaders this couple had a mob of high school kids at their house every Friday night for *Shabbos* dinner. Although they were observant, they lived in Rockville Centre, which did not have a religious Jewish community. On Friday nights, when there were usually no women attendees, the husband would *daven* at B'nai Shalom. On *Shabbos* morning he would walk for an hour to the Young Israel of Oceanside, the closest Orthodox *shul*. The Friday night meal was our first experience as a couple of a real *Shabbos* atmosphere. The food was delicious there was singing and camaraderie. On *Shabbos* morning we drove to B'nai Shalom to attend services and had lunch with the Hymans. Although he was a Conservative Rabbi, Hillel had grown up in an Orthodox home and *shul* in Hartford, Connecticut. He was a "right-wing" Conservative, meaning that he kept the *halachos* of *Shabbos* and *kashruth*, etc. and resisted the innovations that were sweeping the Conservative movement at that time—like counting women in a *minyan* and calling a woman to the Torah. In fact, except for *Shabbos*, the *minyan* he *davened* in at JTS had a *mechitzah*, a barrier separating the men from the women.

Hillel did not agree with the Reform rabbi in matters of marriage and conversion. He questioned my wife about matters of observance, including holidays and *Shabbos* and when he was convinced that she was sincere in her desire to observe what she knew and become a part of the Jewish Nation, he convened a religious court, a *Beis Din* of three observant men, and brought her to the *mikvah* in Far Rockaway for her *tevilah*. We now felt that she was 100% Jewish. Following the conversion, we had a *chuppah* in the *shul* and were married according to Jewish Law, at least as interpreted by the Conservative Movement. My parents made a beautiful wedding reception for us at their home.

Hillel gave a *Talmud* class in the *shul* one evening a week. We joined. It was my first exposure to this ancient text. We were encouraged to analyze the text and ask as many questions as we could think of. I am very inquisitive by nature and at that point in my life rarely agreed with any authority figure. Surprisingly, unlike my secular educational experience, this was a virtue in learning *Talmud.* After a few months Hillel told me that I had a *"gemara kopf"* (a *Talmudic* head), which I thought was a great compliment coming from a professor of *Talmud.* Of course, at that point, I could barely read Hebrew and couldn't read the Talmud by myself, but I loved the classes and the intellectual stimulation of the ancient texts. I thought of becoming a Conservative Rabbi like Hillel. He told me that I would very likely be accepted into JTS. But urged me to think carefully about such a move, since, as we became more observant, we might become Orthodox, and a Conservative rabbi would have no place in the Orthodox world. His prediction came true. As we got more involved in the classes and were exposed more and more to the world of Orthodoxy through our friends at NCSY, I started thinking about going to Yeshiva University—an Orthodox institution and learning to be a rabbi there. There was one problem—my background. I didn't think they would accept me since I had no Hebrew skills. The *Gemara* is written in Aramaic and without punctuation or vowel points. I viewed my lack of skills as almost an insurmountable obstacle. At the same time, I had to think seriously about my future. I knew that rabbis weren't paid much, and it would probably take me at least another four years of intense study to be ordained during which time I wouldn't be able to work. And even if I were successful, why would I be hired over someone who had studied in *yeshiva* all his life?

CHAPTER V
My Choice of Professions

I was also drawn to the legal profession, which seemed to offer a more realistic opportunity to make a living. I had worked in my cousin's general practice law office in Suffolk County as a law clerk during the summer before my junior year of college. I really enjoyed researching the law and writing up my conclusions. But what really attracted me to the profession was my experience with his *pro bono* cases assigned to him by Legal Aid.

I don't remember many of the cases I worked on. They were run of the mill car accidents. But two cases ignited my passion for the profession. The first was a murder.

My cousin and I drove out to Riverhead, the county seat, and met our client at the jailhouse. She was an "exotic dancer"—at least that's what the local newspapers called her. She was white and about twenty-five years old, bleach blonde and quite tall. She was originally from Detroit, where her father was a policeman. She had fallen off the straight and narrow and moved to New York where she took up with a Black drummer whose name was Johnny Berry. He cheated on her, and she shot him dead. While her name wasn't Frankie, she absolutely reminded me of the song. For an eighteen-year-old kid from the staid New York suburbs, this was like a dream come true. It was as if I were an actor in a crime movie or a character in a crime novel. I immediately empathized with her and her plight.

Legally there wasn't much to do. She admitted the act, pleaded guilty to manslaughter and got ten years in prison.

The second case was different. It wasn't like a cheap paperback novel, or a Billie Holiday song. It was an outrageous travesty. Suffolk County at the time was still very rural. There were many farms, and the farmworkers were almost all Mexicans or Central American guest workers. Our clients, three brothers, one dishwasher and two farmworkers from Honduras, were accused of felony assault upon three Suffolk County police officers and a retired wheelchair-bound policeman. They spoke no English and were very frightened. Fortunately for them and my cousin, I spoke Spanish. Suffolk County provided no interpreters at the time. The judge at their arraignment allowed me to interpret for them at their various court appearances.

The story they told inflamed my passion for justice. They were on their way home after work, peaceably walking down a county road one Sunday afternoon, when a van pulled up beside them. Three drunken men, and as it turned out all off-duty cops, screamed ethnic curses, jumped them, and beat them badly. The retired cop in the wheelchair stayed in the van. The same cops who assaulted them arrested them and took them down to the county jail. Over the next seventy-two hours, other policemen with rubber hoses beat them mercilessly. They had black and blue marks all over their faces and bodies. At their arraignment, my cousin asked for a doctor to examine their bruises. His findings were inconclusive. He couldn't tell how the bruises had been inflicted. The brothers had no criminal record and had never been arrested before. I was convinced of their innocence. But they were facing an almost insurmountable challenge—White police officers, defenders of the community, claiming that drunken Latino illegals violently assaulted them for no reason at all. Who would believe these poor Latinos? They couldn't even speak English to defend themselves in court. I did.

After that first meeting I knew what I wanted to do with my life. I would become a criminal lawyer and defend the oppressed and powerless. I don't exactly remember what happened to our clients, but I seem to recall that they plead guilty to a lesser offense and were released on probation after a short jail sentence—which was almost a miracle. How many Blacks or Latinos have rotted away in prison because of false charges manufactured by crooked policemen? Maybe the result had something to do with my cousin's close relationship with the prosecutor. Since Legal Aid cases paid almost nothing to the defense lawyer, it made more sense for my cousin to get a plea bargain from the prosecutor than to spend weeks preparing for a trial that would be a coin flip, with a coin heavily weighted towards "tails you lose". The jury in a conservative county like Suffolk, would have a majority of White, right wing, and probably prejudiced jurors. The outcome would be predictably "guilty."

If I had been their lawyer, I would have convinced my clients to plead "not guilty" and gone to trial. Had I lost, I would have fought their case all the way to the U.S. Supreme Court. I would also have sued the Suffolk County Police Department for millions and not have rested until those racist and sadistic policemen were behind bars. Of course, I know now that I would have most likely failed, but at that time I thought I was invincible.

Although that passion for justice was sufficient for my choice of profession, I was also attracted to the law because I loved to see how things worked. As a kid I would take apart watches or other mechanical devices to see their inner workings. The problem was I could never figure out how to put them together again. The same thing with models. I loved getting a model of a plane or a battleship to assemble. But often, in my enthusiasm, I disregarded the instructions in the box and glued the pieces together in the way I assumed to be correct. The problem was that I was often wrong. Also, I wasn't so good with my hands. I was always putting too much glue on the pieces and smearing it over the surface of the model. Or, while trying to paste the insignia on the front of the model I would tear it or place it in the wrong spot and in trying to fix my mistake, make it worse. My best friend at the time was Johnny, who went on to become an engineer. He was exceedingly neat and could follow instructions to the tee. In an aptitude test that we took in Junior High School, I scored low in spatial relations, which indicated, said the guidance counselor, that I shouldn't consider engineering as a profession.

But I never stopped being interested in how things worked. One of the biggest mysteries to me was how society worked. How did societies organize themselves? How did they regulate themselves? How did they rule themselves? In college I majored in Anthropology and was fascinated by the analysis of the organization of society and the structure of language. But academia was not in the cards for me. Not with the Vietnamese War staring me in the face. By the time I returned to the United States from Spain, I was already twenty-four years old and married. To begin graduate school at that age and then working for maybe ten years to earn a PhD in Anthropology or Linguistics, the two academic areas I was most interested in, and then trying to get a job, seemed as impractical as trying to become an Orthodox pulpit rabbi.

One could say that lawyers are social engineers. They devise and maintain the mechanisms that allow a society to function smoothly. At least that's the way I looked at it. Others, like the revolutionary Dick the Butcher in Shakespeare's Henry VI, would disagree. Dick said: "The first thing we do, let's kill all the lawyers." I suppose that in Elizabethan England that was a common way of thinking. Lawyers subverted the good in society. They manipulated the system for their own benefit first and then for the benefit of their rich clients. And even a few hundred years later, in Dickens' Victorian England, lawyers were pettifogging bumblers who contributed nothing to society, only to their pockets. But I lived in a country with the U.S. Constitution and with it and a pen, one could change society for the better. Or so I thought. And with only three years of schooling, the Legal Profession offered a relatively secure, remunerative, and academic profession that appealed to me.

As I later found out, *Talmudic* training was a major plus for a law student. The teaching method adopted by almost all law schools in America, is the "case method." Students are given actual cases to read and then to analyze. A clear picture of the facts is the first task of the student. The same is true in Talmudic study. The facts often determine the outcome of the case. The *Gemara* cites actual or fictitious sets of facts and goes on to recount the discussions, arguments, and analyzes in the Babylonian *yeshivos* of Sura and Pompidisa, and often decides the *Halacha*.

In 1973, I started law school in Cleveland, Ohio. At the same time, we made the decision to become fully observant Jews.

CHAPTER VI
We Become Frum

My wife's conversions and our increasing participation in Jewish communal life and eventual observance was a slow process. We knew that the goal was to eventually keep all the *mitzvohs*, but never felt that we had to do it all at once. I assumed that *Hashem* would be happy if we moved at a slow pace. And no one told us otherwise. We stopped listening to the radio on the *Shabbos* drive to *shul*; we stopped buying non-kosher food; we stopped eating in non-kosher restaurants and eventually stopped driving on *Shabbos*—everything at our own slow pace. After settling in Cleveland and making the decision to lead a fully Orthodox life, one of our new friends, concerned about the validity of my wife's Conservative conversion, arranged for her to undergo her third and final conversion with three Orthodox rabbis in town. We also married each other for the third time.

My brother Yaacov was much more ideological in his approach to observance. He listened to one of the lecturers at Ohr HaTzadikim, Rabbi Dovid Goodman, who convinced him that the Torah was true—that Hashem spoke to the Jewish People on Mount Sinai and gave us rules to live by. He needed no more convincing and immediately resolved to keep everything. I completely understand this position and think it's the only logical one. But, for some reason or other, at the time I didn't think like that.

This doesn't mean that my belief wasn't also intellectually grounded. I was struck by the astounding improbability of an evolutionary process that produced such a balanced and integrated world without a Creator. This is sometimes known as "The Watchmaker Analogy" or "Intelligent Design."

Some people argue that "Intelligent Design" is not a convincing argument for a scientist. But that's not so. A friend of mine, a physics professor at Case Western Reserve University, told me that the reason he became observant was through his study of color vision. It would seem, according to evolutionary theory, those species higher up on the evolutionary ladder, with larger brains relative to their body mass, would develop more complex functions. Color vision, he told me, is incredibly complex and should logically require a large brain. Yet, some birds, reptiles, fish and even mollusks and invertebrates which have small or tiny brains, have tetrachromatic vision which enables them to detect ultraviolet wavelengths of light that translate in the brain to colors that are invisible to the human eye. Humans and other primates have trichromatic color vision and most mammals have only dichromatic color vision, rendering them essentially colorblind. (An article in the July 2006 issue of *Scientific American* entitled *"What Birds See"* by Dr. Timothy Goldsmith, an emeritus Professor of Biology at Yale University explains the intricacies of color vision). This inexplicable contradiction in evolutionary theory led him to the belief that there must be a Creator.

But what was most convincing to me early on in my religious life was the Torah itself. Leviticus enumerates the laws of *tumah and taharah* – a plethora of rules in minute detail determining whether an object, animal carcass, person or food is ritually pure or impure; what is its level of purity; and how to render pure the impure and the impure, pure. Purity is essential for sacrifices, for eating certain foods, for marital relations, and other aspects of life. Impurity can be imparted by certain physical emissions, contact with people or foods that are *tamei* (impure), or with dead people, dead animals, or certain dead reptiles, or even being in certain proximity or enclosures that are impure. Removing the impurity and being restored to a state of purity has many sets of rules, depending on the level of impurity. If humans wrote the Torah, why would they make up such complicated and irrational rules? One could say, as a doctor friend of mine did when I told him of my argument—"A highly intelligent OCD person could come up with them." Granted. But how would you convince an entire intelligent nation to go along with such craziness if it wasn't Divinely commanded. This argument seems to me to be unassailable.

If we assume that Moshe was the greatest prophet in history and spoke "face to face" with the Holy One, there is no mystery as to why the Jewish Nation accepted these rules. But, if you believe, as the Bible Critics do, that the Torah was not dictated by G-d on Mt. Sinai, rather compiled at different times in Jewish history by different authors, why in the world would Jews accept the rules of *tumah* and *taharah* if they weren't Divine? Does anyone think that Jews are so gullible that some charlatan could come along a thousand years after the Exodus from Egypt and convince the Nation to keep the complicated laws of *tumah* and *taharah* because G-d spoke to him and outlined the rules? More likely, he would be stoned to death as a false prophet since the Torah itself prohibits the addition of new *mitzvohs*. The Torah calls Jews: *"am kishe oref"*—a stiff-necked People. As Rabbi Avigdor Miller was wont to say: "Why did G-d give the Torah to a stubborn and stiff-necked

People? Because if you want words to last you don't carve them in a block of butter, you carve them in marble." Stiff-necked people don't change their behavior or beliefs without incontrovertible evidence.

By the time my wife and I got to Cleveland for law school, we were fully committed to keeping *Shabbos* and *kashrus*. We were what I would call today "*dati leumi*" or "Modern Orthodox". We certainly didn't relate to the "*Yeshiva* world"— the world of black hats, black suits and white shirts and long skirts and *sheitels* (wigs).

Because my Hebrew reading skills at the beginning of my spiritual journey were almost non-existent, I initially didn't *daven* daily with a *minyan*. I couldn't keep up with the pace of the congregation. After my first year of law school, I began attending *minyan* in the morning. There was a forty-five-minute *Gemara shiur* (Talmud class) before *shacharis* (morning prayers) and I started going to that too. It awakened the dormant interest I had in learning *Gemara* with Hillel.

By the start of my third year of law school, Telshe *Yeshiva* had initiated a learning program in Cleveland Heights. Members of the Telshe *Kollel* (the division for married students) would come from Wickliffe, Ohio, the site of the *yeshiva*, a few evenings a week, to learn with *baalei batim* (working men). My first tutor, Izzy, was a great teacher. We started with *Meseches* (Tractate) *Beitza*, which deals with *hilchos yom tov* (the laws of the Holidays). He had me memorize the *shakla v'tariya* (the stream of argument) of each *sugya* (topic) we were learning and would test me on it the next time we met. It was a very rigorous approach to learning *Gemara* and one that appealed to me. I felt I was making progress. After about a year of learning with Izzy, I could see myself, in the far distant future, reaching a level where I might be able to learn a piece of *gemara* on my own.

After two years of learning I completed that tractate and made a festive *siyum* (celebration). I felt good about myself, but also realized how handicapped I really was. If I was ever to get to a level of others my age who had learnt in *yeshiva,* I would have to "up my game". I needed to learn more.

At about this time, the Telshe *Rosh Yeshiva*, Rav Mordechai Gifter, came to the Heights on Sunday mornings to teach the *Sefer HaChinuch* (The Book of *Mitzvohs*) to the community. As he was wont to often quote the anonymous author of this 13th century work (who describes himself only as a "Levite from Barcelona"), the purpose of the book is to give us *taamei hamitzvohs* – "a taste" of the *mitzvohs*. Rav Gifter emphasized that to give a "reason" for a *mitzvah* is impossible, because we have no way of divining the mind of the Almighty. We can only experience a "taste"—an insight into the *mitzvah* that we, on our level, can understand. I cannot describe the impact this man made on me. He spoke to my heart.

Rav Gifter was born in Richmond, Virginia and never lost the slight trace of a Southern accent. He was a brilliant orator. I am sure that had he decided to go into politics instead of the rabbinate, he would have been the most eloquent Senator in the U.S. Congress. I can still hear his stentorian voice exclaiming, "If we believe there is a Commander, then we must follow his command." This experience of hearing Rav Gifter's voice in my head, even today, is not only my own. Almost anyone who heard him years ago can still hear him now.

CHAPTER VII
The Decision to Move to Israel

After law school I worked for a corporate law firm in Cleveland, where I was the only Jew. Two years later I started my own practice. I worked very hard for about eight years – expanding the areas of practice by bringing in other lawyers and partners. At the age of 37, when a mid-life crisis is quite common, I was also at a crossroads in my practice. Some of my colleagues had given up the law and gone into teaching or painting or decided to sail around the world. Other friends quit their medical practices and became plumbers and others had divorced their wives and married girls young enough to be their daughters.

For a couple of years prior to our *Aliyah*, I had been leaving the office in the late afternoon and going to Telshe Yeshiva to learn *Gemara* for a couple of hours. But because I was the managing partner of the firm, I had a thousand things on my mind day and night and could never devote my full concentration to my learning. I was also in court almost every day and that required preparation and great attention to detail. Learning Torah and especially *gemara* requires a clear head and extreme focus. I realized that if I was ever going to achieve my goal of gaining competence in my learning there was only one solution for me. I had to learn full time in *yeshiva* in a new environment totally removed from my life in Cleveland. I decided that moving to Israel and going to *yeshiva* was something I needed to do. If not, I didn't think I could live with myself. I would always feel that I had robbed myself of the greatest treasure—and the dream and prayer of my great-grandmother, *Nani-Nani,* who sang to me in Yiddish when I was a little boy of the Torah being the *beste sechora*—the best merchandise in the world.

I had several reasons for moving to Israel when I did. One was the influence of the Rabbi of our *shul,* Rabbi Shubert Spero. Apart from being the rabbi of the Young Israel of Cleveland, he was also a philosophy professor at Case Western Reserve University. Rabbi Spero was an ardent religious Zionist. This was unusual for someone with his "black hat" *yeshiva* background. He was not a Yeshiva University graduate—a decidedly Zionistic institution, but an alumnus of Torah v'Daas, a traditional right-wing *yeshiva* in Brooklyn. Rabbi Spero was a passionate advocate of *Aliyah.* In almost every *drasha* (speech) he gave on Shabbos morning, he related the *Parsha* (the weekly Torah portion) to the *mitzvah* of *Yishuv haAretz*—settling in Israel.

Here we were in the latter part of the 20th century. The miracle of the birth of the State of Israel in 1948 was a very recent event. For 2000 years we Jews were bereft of a Homeland. The longing for our return was encrypted in every prayer. During and at the end of every holiday Jews proclaim: *"L'shana Haba'ah B'yerushalayim"*—Next year in Jerusalem! After two millennia, we still remembered the destruction of Jerusalem and the Temple every day through our prayers and many times a year through our fasting. The Land of Israel was a holy place that awaited the faithful—a barren land that bloomed when the Jews returned to it, exactly as promised by the Prophets. While over the millennia, a handful of very pious individuals had braved the dangers of pirates and bandits just to get to the Holy Land, what awaited them?—A life of hardship and poverty, marauding Crusaders and Arabs. And now we had the opportunity to fly there in safety in less than twelve hours. Our Homeland is a place where many of the commandments of the Torah can only be performed, and we can live in beautiful homes with all the modern conveniences. We can find jobs and excellent education for our children and fulfill the dreams of our ancestors. Who could say "no" to this G-d given opportunity? Rabbi Spero heeded his own advice and moved to Israel in 1983, where he is a professor of Philosophy at Bar Ilan University. His children and their families soon followed. They were close friends of ours. Other close friends also made *Aliyah* before we did. My best friend from Law School, Yanky Weissman, got a job as a lawyer with Israel Aircraft Industries, one of the largest companies in Israel. Another friend, Simcha Seligman, found work as an accountant with the Israeli office of an international accounting firm. The fact that our closest friends were making *Aliyah*, made our decision that much easier.

When a religious Jewish Agency *shaliach* (agent) and his wife moved to Cleveland, we, along with many friends, attended regular meetings to prepare us for *Aliyah*. They discussed the practical aspects of the move—what furniture and appliances we should buy and pack in our lift, schooling for children, neighborhoods, etc., etc.

Now that I felt like a part of the Telshe Yeshiva, I wanted the approval of my *Rosh Yeshiva*, Rav Gifter, to whom I had grown increasingly close. Years before, the great Cleveland philanthropist, Mr. Irving Stone, donated money to build a religious settlement and a branch of the Telshe Yeshiva on the outskirts of Jerusalem in partnership with the Israeli branch of the Telshe Yeshiva Sorotzkin family, called Kiryat Telshe Stone. Rav Gifter was asked by the *Yeshiva* to move to Israel to become its *Rosh HaYeshiva* there, while his co-*Rosh HaYeshiva*, Rav Boruch Sorotzkin was to remain in Cleveland. When Rav Boruch died, the *Yeshiva* family asked Rav Gifter to return to Cleveland to resume his leadership there. He didn't want to leave *Eretz Yisroel*, but he felt the decision wasn't his alone to make. He asked the *Godol Hador*, The Steipler Rov – the leader of the Lithuanian Yeshivos in Israel, what he should do. The Steipler told him that he had to return. The leadership of the Telshe Yeshiva had precedence over Rav Gifter's personal reasons for staying in the Holy Land. Rav Gifter cried. He didn't want to go back, but what could he do? *Daas Torah* (the Voice of Torah) had spoken.

While Rabbi Spero was an inspiring and enthusiastic Zionist and based his arguments for *Aliyah* on *halacha* and the fulfillment of Prophecy, Rabbi Gifter was a poetic Zionist. He had a burning love for the Land.

Although he returned to Wickliffe, Ohio, he could never reconcile himself to living in *Chutz L'aretz* (outside the Land). He refused to return to his house on Yeshiva Lane but moved with his wife into the dormitory. I visited with him there on several occasions. He had preserved flowers indigenous to Eretz Yisroel and kept them on prominent display in the dining area of his living room. He showed them to every visitor and waxed poetic about the red and purple *kalanit* and *rakefet*. He would reminisce about his life in the Holy Land. Every morning after *shacharis* in the *Yeshiva* in Telshe Stone, he would stroll for half an hour through the forest of the settlement accompanied by the *bochurim* (unmarried *yeshiva* students) of the *Yeshiva*, pointing out to them the different flora and fauna and speaking of the beauty of *Eretz Yisroel*. One year, after returning to Wickliffe from a winter vacation in Miami Beach, he was shocked to find carpeting on the floor of his apartment in the dorm. Some well-meaning alumni thought to make his living conditions cozier and had the carpet installed while he was gone. He ordered it removed immediately, saying, "What were they thinking? If I wanted to live in a dwelling with carpeting I would have moved back to my house. I live in the dorm because I can't live in a *diras kevah* (a permanent house) in *chutz L'aretz*, only in *Eretz Yisroel*. This is a *diras aray* (a temporary dwelling). And a *diras aray* doesn't have carpeting."

Rav Gifter's love of *Eretz Yisroel* was infectious and spoke to my heart. However, he was also a realist and insisted that I have a plan before I go. I needed a certain amount of money – enough to buy an apartment and sustain the family while I learnt. But at the same time, he was also very encouraging of the idea of my going to learn in *yeshiva*.

One might think that as a *Rosh Yeshiva* he might encourage everyone who was so inclined to learn Torah in Israel to move. But that's not true. I know of many other young men—*Kollel* members, professionals, or businessmen whom he told not to move—their place was in America, and they should continue learning and working there. His advice hinged on many factors. Americans, even those living on government assistance, as many *Kollel* members did, expected a certain standard of living. Israel is a poorer country and government benefits were much more modest than in the States. Even if the husband would be willing to live in poverty to learn Torah in Israel, his wife and children might not. Therefore, a sizable nest egg, or guaranteed support from family members would be required. Eventually, almost all young men learning in *Kollel* must work to support their growing families and to marry off their children. The need in Israel for native English-speaking rabbis or teachers is extremely limited. A different avenue for earning a living would then be required. Very few American *Kollel* men have those employable skills or education. However, those same young men might have very bright and rewarding careers as pulpit rabbis or *rebbes* in day schools and *yeshivos* in North America. Depending on the ages, sex and nature of the children, advice about moving will differ. Some kids are easily adaptable to new environments and others aren't. Some are friendly and easy to make friends with, others are shy and withdrawn. If you remove some children from a comfortable environment to one in which they feel and are made to feel like outsiders, they can be traumatically impacted. The same applies to the wife and husband. These are a few reasons why a *rov* may encourage some to make *Aliyah* and others not. Rav Gifter, *z"l,* who had great insight into his students, tailored his advice accordingly.

Another influential factor in our *Aliyah* was that my partners hadn't been happy that I was spending more time away from the office. Because I was not going to abandon my serious attempt at Torah learning, I could see that in the not-too-distant future, things would come to a head.

But possibly the biggest factor in my decision, and one that I kept to myself, was a change I noticed in me. The Jewish People have three forefathers: *Avraham* (Abraham), *Yitzchok* (Isaac) and *Yaacov* (Jacob). Each one has endowed the Jewish People with a particular trait. Avraham's was *chesed* (kindness); Yitzchok's was *gevurah* (strength—unwavering devotion to G-d); and Yaacov's was *emes*—truth). Jews are supposed to be distinguished by those characteristics. While I was probably weak in the first two, I didn't notice it as much as I did the third. A lawyer is supposed to be a zealous advocate for his client. In a courtroom, or in negotiations with an opposing party, the lawyer's job is to present his client's position in the most favorable light. In a courtroom setting, where a witness might take the stand and testify, it means preparing him to smartly answer anticipated questions and attacks. In a negotiation, it might mean puffing or bluffing. Not outright lying, G-d forbid, but exaggerating the truth. In my mind this is not what the Prophet meant when he said: *"titain emes l'Yaacov"*—"give truth to Yaacov"—meaning Jews should be truthful (Micah 7:20), or as it says in the Torah: *"m'dvar sheker tirchak"*—*"keep far away from untruth."* (Exodus 23:7).

The problem wasn't so much that I was being a zealous advocate for my client, but that after years of doing so, it was affecting my interactions with everyone else. I found myself stretching the truth, even when there was no foreseeable benefit to myself or anyone else. My personality was changing, and it frightened me. The time to move was now.

We decided we would be able to move within about a year and applied for *Aliyah*. In November of 1985, our son, Binyamin Tzvi, named for my deceased father, was born. This was a momentous occasion. Prior to his birth we had two girls. As many fathers do, I was hoping for a male heir—someone to carry on our family name; and someone to say *kaddish* (the prayer for the dead) for me when I'm gone. A father has a *mitzvah* to bring his son into the Covenant with a *bris milah* (circumcision) on the eighth day of his life. It is accompanied by a festive meal and speeches. I was excited. I had asked a good friend of mine who was an experienced *mohel* (circumciser) to be my agent and perform the procedure in front of a large crowd of friends and family. Five days before the event another close friend of mine, Jonathan, urged me to perform the mitzvah myself.

"You know" Jonathan told me, "It says in the *Gemara* that it's preferable to do a mitzvah yourself rather than do it through a *shaliach* (an agent)" (*Kiddushin* 41a).

"Yes. I'm aware of that, but who does a *bris milah* on his son? Everyone uses a *mohel.* "

"Well," he said, "I did it for my three sons."

"That's all well and good my friend, but you're a urologist. I'm sure you probably practiced on hundreds of non-Jewish babies before you did your own kids. I'm just a lawyer and never did anything remotely connected to an operation."

"It's true that I have practice, but I'm telling you there's nothing to it."

"Easy for you to say," I answered.

"No, really, it's easy. The consistency of the foreskin is very similar to that of raw chicken. I'll give you a scalpel and a shield. You have another five days to practice. You'll see it's easy to do and you'll be doing the mitzvah in the best way possible."

It's a good thing for me that my wife is so easy going. When I told her about my plan, she didn't discourage me. On the contrary she was only sorry that she wouldn't be doing it herself.

On the day of the *bris,* I had my friend, the *mohel,* at my side to assist me in case something went wrong or in case I fainted. To my surprise and great satisfaction, I did a perfect job. Testimony to my success is that my son now has three boys and one girl.

We made *Aliyah* before Binyamin Tzvi's first birthday.

To accomplish my financial goals, I had to sell my interest in the firm to my partners. Even if I could convince them that they should pay me for my share in the partnership, the value of a partnership minus the founder and managing partner is not a simple calculation. Determining a formula for the buyout was complicated. Fortunately for me, my partners were Mid-Westerners and believed in fairness and preserving a good relationship. In the end we reached an amicable settlement that none of us were a hundred percent happy with, but we all recognized as fair. It enabled me to come to *Eretz Yisroel* with the nest egg that Rabbi Gifter recommended and his blessing. I could learn without needing to work for several years. I would now be a self-supporting *Kollel* man.

CHAPTER VIII
A New Language

I was coming from the country and language of my birth to a foreign land filled with people who, although we shared a common religion and much DNA, were very different from me. The language and culture of Israel was going to be a challenge. I can't say that I was enamored of the few Israelis I had met. They seemed to live up to their stereotype of being loud, strongly opinionated and not as polite as the people I had known in Cleveland. But they were friendly—maybe a bit too friendly. In our first week in Israel while traveling on the public buses, we saw firsthand examples. Israelis thought nothing of criticizing their fellow travelers' poor parenting skills because they dressed their kids in clothing too warm for the season. In the winter it was the opposite. I assumed that because Israelis view each other as family, they couldn't remain silent when viewing a violation of their family's ethics or philosophy or code of conduct. Such familiarity and lack of tact made me uncomfortable.

As to language, I was a lawyer who had mastered the mechanics and language of American law. I was now in a country whose language I didn't speak and whose legal system was quite different. If I were to practice law in Israel, I'd be at a very significant disadvantage. I was now the "greener"—the newly arrived immigrant who makes serious grammatical mistakes and expresses himself clumsily. My children would laugh at my attempts to speak Hebrew. There is a story I heard about a young American seminary girl in Jerusalem who wanted a round trip ticket to Tel Aviv. She gets onto the bus and says to the driver *"Ani chazira"*. ("I'm a pig"). The whole bus erupts in laughter. She meant to say: *"ani achzor"*—"I am returning. I'd like a round-trip ticket." I was afraid that I'd make a stupid mistake like she did. I'm still afraid.

I thought and wrote in English. Prior to law school I had lived in Spain for almost three years. Because of my total immersion in that language and culture, I would think and even dream in Spanish, yet I still had problems reading the newspaper (which my wife tells me was done purposely during the Franco regime so that no one could understand what was really happening in the country). It was difficult for me to read books in Spanish, because literary writing is quite different from the spoken language. And I made grammatical mistakes. I didn't think I was going to get as far in Hebrew as I did in Spanish. I was much older now and my brain was not as supple as it was when I was twenty-one. Also, after years of listening to music at a high volume, my sense of hearing—extremely important in learning a language—was dulled. Another impediment was that the neighborhood in which we were living had an overwhelming majority of English speakers. I was entering a *yeshiva* where the teaching was largely in English and most of the students were from English speaking countries. And, of course, we spoke English at home with our kids. I didn't think I would ever be able to express myself as fluently or as intelligently in Hebrew as in English or even Spanish.

While my reading comprehension in Biblical and Talmudic Hebrew and Aramaic was passable, I had never spoken Hebrew. So, I decided to take an *Ulpan*—a course in Hebrew Language, which was offered free of charge to new immigrants. I enrolled in an intensive two-month *Ulpan* at Hebrew University. Because of my reading comprehension I placed into a higher-level Hebrew course, where everyone else could chatter away in that language, whereas I stumbled my ungrammatical way through a simple sentence.

The *Ulpan* was an interesting introduction into the Israeli world. The students, of course, weren't Israeli and of the twenty or so that were in the class, eight of them were Catholic nuns and priests from Korea. The rest were young men and women mostly from Europe, with a few from the English-speaking world. The two teachers, male and female, were Israelis. They were the first real Israelis that I got to know in Israel. Doron was non-religious, and I couldn't tell if Orit was religious or not. She didn't cover her hair and sometimes wore slacks. While in the religious world that I had known, that would have strongly indicated a non-religious lifestyle, in Israel I knew that the differences were subtler. I started the course in early August, during what is known as the "Three Weeks"—or in Yiddish, the *"Dri Vachen"*. These are the three weeks before Tisha B'Av—the 9th of the month of Av, the saddest day in the Jewish calendar, when both the First and Second Temples were destroyed. Tisha B'Av is a 24-hour fast day. To set the mood for this period of the year, from the 17th of Tammuz (when the walls of Jerusalem were breached by the enemy) until Tisha B'Av—the ninth of the month of Av, the Ashkenazi rabbis forbade listening to music, making weddings, shaving and getting haircuts.

When Orit was going to teach us a song, she hinted to me that I might like to leave the class, knowing that religious men are forbidden to listen to a woman singing.

The Hebrew University campus is on *Har Hatzofim* (Mount Scopus), which is also known as *Har Hazaitim*, the Mount of Olives. After class I would daven *mincha* in the Hecht Synagogue at the University and then return home

The synagogue has a huge floor to ceiling glass window, which overlooks the very nearby Temple Mount. The view is breathtaking. The Golden Dome of the Rock, a Moslem Holy site, is massive and, as its name implies, is coated in gold leaf. It shines brightly in the daytime and dominates the Old City skyline. "The Rock" is the altar upon which Avraham bound Isaac and raised his knife to sacrifice him.

CHAPTER IX
The Yeshiva

After completing the *Ulpan*, I entered Ohr HaTzadikim Yeshiva at the beginning of the Winter *zmam* (term) 5747 (1986).

On my first day of *Yeshiva*, I received what I thought was a perk of being an *Avreich* (a married Torah student). When I opened the front door of our apartment, I found hanging on the door handle a bag of six freshly baked and still warm *lachmaniot* (bread rolls). As there were five of us in the family, this Manna from Heaven was obviously the gift of some generous benefactor who wanted to help poor married *yeshiva* students feed their families. Since I had an income, I didn't want to take the charity that could be given to someone more needy. That evening, I wrote a note in Hebrew, put it in the bag with the rolls and tied it to the door handle. It said, "Thank you very much for your kindness, but we don't need these *lachmaniot*, please give them to a poor family."

I wasn't sure how the anonymous benefactor had gotten my name, but I figured that he or she must have access to the registry of students in the *Yeshiva*.

The next morning the old bag and note were gone, but new fresh and warm *lachmanio*t were hanging in their place. That night I left another note on the door—this time in English, but in the morning another bag of *lachmanio*t appeared. This continued every day. I tried getting up extra early to see who our benefactor might be, but he or she always eluded me. I thought that whoever it was must be a great *tzadik (a* righteous person). I had read about *Mar Ukvah*, one of the great Sages in the Talmud and his wife, who would give *tzedakah* (charity) secretly. One day a poor man ran after them to see who his anonymous benefactor might be. The rabbi and his wife ran into a large, burning baker's oven to avoid being seen. When they emerged and were asked how they could have survived the burning oven, the rabbi said it was in the merit of *tzedakah*. But, he explained, his wife's merit was greater than his. To avoid burning his feet, he stood on hers. Why didn't her feet burn? Because he only gave money anonymously to the poor, while she prepared and delivered food to their doorsteps and ran away before they opened the door. I thought that our *lachmaniot* benefactor must be copying that great Sage's wife. (*Kesuvos* 16b).

After a month passed, as I opened the new bag of *lachmaniot,* I saw a note inside. I eagerly opened it up. It was a bill for 300 shekels from a local bakery. Another lesson learned. "There's no such thing as a free breakfast."

At that time the *Yeshiva* had an English Program for the English speakers and a Hebrew Program for Israelis. I decided that I would join the Israeli program so that I could practice my newly acquired Hebrew. My first c*havrusah* (learning partner) was a fluent Hebrew speaker from Argentina. We studied in Hebrew.

I was placed in the *shiur* (class) of Rav Amram Blackman, the *Rosh Yeshiva* (the Head of the *Yeshiva)*. The *shiur* was in Hebrew. Rav Amram was known in the *Yeshiva* World as the Prince of *Seder Nashim*—one of the six orders of the *Talmud*.

One of the greatest Torah personalities in the world at the time, he was a genius with a photographic memory and was a brilliant thinker. He was also a kindly grandfather figure to all his *talmidim*. Born in Soviet Russia in 1921, he and his family managed to escape in 1930 and came to Tel Aviv. At the age of twelve he entered the Hebron Yeshiva in Jerusalem, the preeminent Lithuanian *Yeshiva* in Israel.

Rav Elimelech Scharf, one of the *Godolei haDor* (the leaders of the generation) chose Reb Amram to be his son-in-law. Here is the story I heard.

In 1948 there was a *Kennesia Gedola of Agudas Yisroel* in Jerusalem (The World Congress of *Agudas Yisroel*). Rav Scharf came from Belgium for the event and was invited to give a lecture to the Hebron Yeshiva. *Shiurim* (classes or lectures) generally begin by asking a seemingly unanswerable question on the text of the *Gemara* and then proceeding to answer it—showing the depth of the text and its commentaries and the methodical and original thinking of the *rebbe*—the lecturer.

Reb Elimelech asked a question. The young Amram immediately interrupted him—questioning the basic assumption of the question. This was unheard of—a *bochur* (an unmarried student) telling the *Gadol HaDor,* that his question was not a real question. Reb Elimelech ignored him and continued with the lecture. Amram got up immediately and walked out of the *Beis Medrash*. After finishing the *shiur* Reb Elimelech asked one of the *talmidim* who was it that asked the question and walked out? He was told that it was Amram Blackman. Reb Elimelech then asked the *talmid* to take him to Amram's dorm room. To understand the significance of his request, imagine the King of England asking to be shown to the quarters of an insolent private in Buckingham Palace who showed disrespect to the King. Instead of berating Amram for his insolence, Reb Elimelech apologized to Amram that he didn't answer his question and explained that the question had thrown him off balance. He had prepared the lecture for many hours and thought that the question he posed was one that needed an answer and then proceeded to work out that answer. When Amram challenged him, he didn't know how to answer, so he ignored him and continued. But after he thought about it, he realized that Amram was right. His question was not a question.

He asked Amram why he walked out. He answered, "I couldn't listen to your analysis seeing that it was based on a false premise."

On the spot, Reb Elimelech asked him if he was engaged. He wasn't. After making inquiries into his character, Reb Elimelech offered him a *shidduch* with his daughter. It was coupled with an invitation to become a *rebbe* in his *yeshiva* in Antwerp and together build his *yeshiva*. Amram accepted. The marriage didn't last. Eventually they divorced and Reb Amram moved back to Israel and remarried.

As with many apocryphal stories, some question its veracity. They say that Reb Elimelech would never have continued his lecture under such a false premise. That may be, but the story does contain one incontrovertible fact—Reb Amram was fearless in his approach to the truth of Torah, and even as a *bochur* was unafraid of questioning a *Gadol HaDor*.

I can personally attest to Reb Amram's remarkable powers of concentration and his photographic memory. He would always look up every reference he quoted in a *shiur* and read from the text. Once, he asked one of the *talmidim* to bring him a certain *sefer* (book) of Rabbi Akiva Eiger. The student came back after five minutes and reported that he couldn't locate it.

Reb Amram leaned back in his chair, closed his eyes and for the next ten minutes it looked as if he was reading the text which was printed on his retina. Later that day I checked the *sefer*. As best as I could remember what he said, it seemed to me that he quoted three printed pages verbatim. On a trip back to Cleveland I recounted this incident to a friend of mine, a rabbi, who had studied under Reb Amram at *Bais HaTorah*, another *yeshiva* in Jerusalem that he founded.

"You think that's impressive?" my friend said. "He can quote word for word from memory any *sefer* or even a manuscript that he read once!"

I would be lying if I said I understood most of what Reb Amram said in those first seven months that I was in the *Yeshiva*. Maybe I understood forty percent. But I tried. Years later I received *smicha* (rabbinic ordination) from Reb Amram.

CHAPTER X
Students of Ohr HaTzakikim

What initially impressed me about Ohr HaTzadikim was both the quality of the *rabbeim* and its students. Many *talmidim* were absolutely brilliant, others were inspiring, and all were extraordinary. Here's a sample of a few of them.

Yaacov Morgenstern

One of the first people I met at Ohr HaTzadikim was twenty-eight-year-old Yaacov. Yaacov had graduated from Harvard Law School about six years earlier and was working for a prestigious Wall Street law firm in their Mergers and Acquisitions department. He was on the fast track to a partnership, which meant professional success and a very high income. He didn't come from a religious home and had no formal Jewish education. A few years earlier he had become interested in Judaism and decided that to properly prepare himself for marriage and the rest of his life, he needed to learn in *yeshiva*. He asked his firm for a year's leave of absence, which was highly unconventional, but they agreed—an obvious testimonial to his skills and potential. With the guidance of his mentoring rabbis, he chose to learn in Ohr HaTzadikim because of its reputation as being a place for serious and hard-working students who wanted to make rapid progress in learning.

Toward the end of his first year, when he realized that one year wouldn't be enough time to accomplish his goals, he asked for and was given a second year of absence. One warm autumn day early in his first year at the *Yeshiva*, I saw him at *mincha* in the *Beis Medrash* with a heavy winter coat and scarf. After *davening* I asked him how he was feeling. He looked feverish and run down. He told me it was just a bad cold and nothing to worry about. I suggested that he take a nap between *mincha* and the afternoon *seder*, which would start in another hour and a half. He looked at me with incredulous horror and said, "I only have a year to learn. I need every minute."

After his second year at the *Yeshiva*, Yaacov profusely thanked his firm for giving him the opportunity to study but that he had decided that he needed still more years in *yeshiva* and wouldn't be returning. He also realized that if he wanted to be a devoted husband and engaged father, he needed a job that would allow him more time with his family than a partner at a major Wall Street firm is afforded. After four years at the *Yeshiva*, Yaacov married and became the general counsel and minor partner in a large New York real estate company owned by a wealthy Orthodox Jewish family. He did well enough there to retire after a few years and has been learning full time in a large East Coast *yeshiva* community for the last thirty years, where he and his wife are raising a large and very observant Jewish family.

Dovid Sunshine

Dovid came to the *Yeshiva* a year after I did. He was placed in the same *shiur* that I was then attending. We were both "older students", I was in my late thirties and Dovid, in his middle forties. Both of us were semi-retired. The *rebbe* felt that we would make a good *chavrusa* (learning pair). He was right.

In a way, a *chavrusa* is like a marriage. As it says about the creation of Eve and her subsequent marriage to Adam:

"And Hashem said, it's not good for Adam to be alone, I will make him an *ezer k'negdo*." (Bereshis 2:18):

That phrase, ezer *k'negdo*, is usually translated into English as "helpmate". But, as *Rashi*, explains, those two words are opposites: "if he is worthy, she is his *ezer* – helpmate", if not, she's his *k'negdo* – his violent opponent, which might be an apt description of marriage between male and female. When the husband is acting properly in all areas of life, the marriage is a joyous partnership. On the other hand…

Rashi's description is applicable to a marriage between male and female. But where there are two normal males it's mostly "*k'negdo*"—a real competition. Like rams butting heads. Do the fighting rams hate each other? Or are they good friends just wanting to sharpen their skills? I don't know. After thirty-five years we're still butting heads, fighting every day about how to understand what we're learning, but there is no question that our love for each other is real. We're both interested in the welfare of our partner.

Dovid is very smart with a big appetite. He told me that when he was in third grade his mother told him that if he got all "A's in school, she would give him whatever he would like as a present. At the end of June of that year, he proudly showed his mother the report card with all "A's. The reward he requested was a whole chicken, which he ate at one sitting. That was much more impressive to me than his grades.

Dovid never graduated from high school. He was accepted

to Harvard and Columbia after his junior year of high school. He chose Columbia because it was closer to his home in Westchester, and more importantly, because Boston had no sit-down kosher delicatessens. At the end of his freshman year of college, his father died suddenly of a heart attack at the age of forty-two. Dovid was only sixteen. He moved back home to help with the family's jewelry business. He commuted to Columbia. After graduation he married Emily and took over the management of the business.

As with many idealists, the Six Day War was the catalyst for David and his wife's decision to make *Aliyah*. He sold his business to his cousin and now had enough capital to start business afresh in Israel. Shortly before they made *Aliyah*, he and Emily had become *baalei teshuva,* but not yet *yeshivish.* They moved to Ramat Gan, next to the Diamond Exchange, where he set up an office. He traveled the world selling diamonds and other precious stones. An Ohr HaTzadikim fundraiser, who came regularly to his office for donations, convinced Dovid to attend classes at an Ohr HaTzadikim branch in Tel Aviv. As he got more involved in learning Torah, he spent his afternoons at a *yeshiva* in nearby *Bnei Braq*. At the age of forty, he decided to sell his business for a tidy sum, retire and learn Torah all day. After a few years he and his family moved to Jerusalem where he learnt in various *yeshivos* ending up eventually in Ohr HaTzadikim. His income now depended on loans and investments.

One investment was in a company, B"H Investments (BHI) that bought "paper" from manufacturers. In the old days, before credit cards were common in Israel, appliance manufacturers would finance the consumer purchases of their wares. A buyer would go into an appliance store and buy a refrigerator. But, as he didn't have the cash to pay for it, he would give a series of post-dated checks made out to the manufacturer for the full price, spread out over three, four or five years. To raise money to run the factory and produce more refrigerators, the manufacturer sold the checks, at a discounted rate, to an investor.

As an example, let's say the fridge cost $300 to produce and the commission to the owner of the appliance store was $50 and the retail price of the fridge was $1000. The manufacturer could sell the post-dated checks to an investor, like BHI, for $500 and the investor would collect the $1000 over the course of the next five years. BHI's return would be 20% per year, a good deal more than it could get in a bank. Of course, there are risks. A certain number of the checks would become bad debts if the buyer defaulted, but, for many years, the default rate in Israel was low. It seemed like a good deal for everyone involved.

Dovid had loaned a great deal of money—representing a sizable chunk of his nest egg—to BHI, a partnership of two brothers who were also religious Jews. As such, they observed the Jewish Laws pertaining to loaning and borrowing money. One of the *mitzvohs* in the Torah is to lend money to your Jewish brethren (Deuteronomy 15: 7–8) and another is not to take any interest from him (Deuteronomy 23:19). In the agricultural society that existed at the time the Torah was given, no one borrowed money for an investment in discounted paper or post-dated checks. You borrowed because you had nothing to eat or because you needed money to buy a field, a bull to plow with, other farm implements, or seed for your field.

Even though it is permissible to rent out your farm equipment, like your plow or your oxen for recompense, or to lease your farmland to a sharecropper for a percentage of his harvest, the Torah does not permit you to loan your money or your food at interest. I heard from my *rebbe*, Rav Moshe Shapiro, *z"l*, that there is nothing intrinsically wrong with earning interest on your money, it's an asset, much like any physical asset, but Hashem wants us to understand that just as He lends us everything in life for free—our lives, our air, our water, our happiness, and if we look deeper—all our assets and possessions, our talents and our families—so too does he want us to imitate Him and to loan certain things to others at no interest. When your brother needs money to survive or to succeed in life, when things aren't going well for him financially, lend it to him for free, just like Hashem does to us.

Although this *mitzvah* applies only to Jews and one may lend to non-Jews at interest, many Jews and Jewish Loan societies extend the idea of the *mitzvah* to non-Jews. When I was a sophomore in university, I had an Anthropology professor, Dr. Margaret Wheeler, who in a lecture about the structure of Jewish community of Toronto, mentioned that support of the poor through interest free loans was a particularly distinguishing characteristic. She related to us that when she was a poor graduate student in Toronto, her landlord, a religious Jew, noticed her dire situation and offered her an interest free loan. Thirty years later she was still praising that man and his religion for being so concerned and so generous to a poor non-Jewish graduate student.

Two thousand years ago, after we lost our Temple and were subsequently exiled from our land by the Romans, agriculture, as a means of making a living, was no longer an option for most Jews. In many countries in Europe and the Middle East, Jews were forbidden to own land or enter certain guilds or professions. So, we went into business—buying and selling, trading, importing, and exporting. We became peddlers, storekeepers, middlemen and moneylenders. As a result, money was not just a means of survival, but also the stock in trade of our businesses. The rabbis were called upon to help avoid the many prohibitions against paying and receiving interest on loans. They were up to the task and invented the *Heter Iska*, which designates part of the amount given to the borrower as a loan and part as an investment.

Dovid's investment in BHI was based on a *Heter Iska* – half was a designated a loan and half an investment. Let's say the total amount that Dovid placed in BHI was $50,000. Under this agreement, $25,000 was a loan, which according to Jewish law cannot carry any interest and must be repaid and another $25,000 was an investment. BHI hoped to return to David a profit of $50,000 by the end of five years. To do so it needed to pay Dovid $75,000 for his share in the partnership and to also return to him his $25,000 loan. For Dovid to receive $75,000 on his original designated investment of $25,000, the rate of return on the investment would be a hefty 12.21% per year compounded annually.

Since BHI was doing all the investing and management of the business, when it came to divvying up the profits, Dovid didn't want to have to trust BHI's numbers, so the *Heter Iska* stipulated that BHI would agree that in lieu of an accounting of the profits of the business, BHI would pay Dovid $75,000 for his investment share—no questions asked.

However, BHI also had the right to tell Dovid that it lost money on the investment and couldn't pay him anything. But for BHI to claim that loss it had to show Dovid certified accounting statements from a professional accountant attesting to the loss and the partners would have to take a "severe oath" in front of a *Beis Din* while holding a *sefer Torah* and swearing on it that they were telling the truth about the loss at pain of extreme consequences. In any case, BHI would still be on the hook for the $25,000 loan.

Well, Dovid's investment in the company went south. The principals claimed that because of an economic downturn in the country, a great many debtors were in default and their checks were uncollectable. As a result, they were losing a great deal of money, and could no longer pay Dovid anything. According to the terms of the *Heter Iska* they had audited statements from a professional accountant and were willing to take the severe oath required by the rabbis. They would continue to pay the loan portion of the *Heter Iska* as best as they could, but to do so they needed to find employment, as their business was bankrupt. Since their skills as financial consultants were not in great demand, they took menial jobs as salesclerks at an appliance store. Their monthly payments to Dovid were a pittance. Dovid's loan and investment was almost a total loss.

Most people in that situation would probably tear their hair out and go into a deep depression. They might even try to contact the Israeli mafia to threaten physical harm to those principals and try to squeeze out whatever money might have squirreled away in some safe deposit box or mattress. Or they might want their pound of flesh and hire a contract killer to "bump off" the offenders. But after exhausting all legal means of trying to collect his debt or to find any indication of malfeasance, Dovid accepted his fate with total equanimity and said: "Hashem decreed that I lose this money and there's no reason for me to feel depressed or to worry about it. Whatever Hashem does is for the best. I'll live with it." And he did.

When he occasionally is reminded of his misadventure, his reaction is the same: "Hashem decreed that I lose the money so there's nothing to think about. As the Sage, Ben Zoma, says in *Pirkei Avos* (Ethics of the Fathers 4:1): 'Who is wealthy? The one who is happy with his lot.'" Although Dovid lost a fortune, because of his faith, his wealth remained intact.

Henry Robinson

Ohr HaTzadikim doesn't only cater to the students with little or no religious background. It also serves those young Jews from religious homes who have drifted away from their heritage and become less observant or even completely secular. Traditional religious Jewish Day Schools and *Yeshivos* in the English-speaking world must provide a dual curriculum—religious and secular studies. That means the school day can be very long. By 3:00 p.m. the typical day school student is counting the minutes until 6:00 p.m. when he can go home and eat dinner and do his homework. There is very little time for diversions and extra-curricular activity for a conscientious student. At many day schools the emphasis is on secular studies and getting accepted at Ivy League or elite colleges. Religious studies take a back seat.

Henry Robinson attended a modern Orthodox day school in Philadelphia where he excelled academically but chafed at the strict rules and rote religious education. He concentrated on his secular studies. After graduating high school at sixteen he started college at the University of Pennsylvania. By the end of his sophomore year, he realized that the very secular campus life was taking a huge toll on what remained of his *Yiddishkeit*, so he decided to transfer to Columbia, where there was a stronger Orthodox student community. He also decided to take a year off to go to a *yeshiva* in Israel with other day school kids of his age. He was underwhelmed and uninspired by his experience at the *yeshiva* and wasn't sorry, when after a few months of coming late to *davening* in the morning, he was expelled. He then joined the foreign students' program at Bar Ilan University. There he majored in what he describes as "Marine Biology"—spending his days at the Tel Aviv beaches trying to pick up girls. His understanding of the underpinnings of Jewish philosophy and his *Gemara* skills did not improve over that year.

At Columbia, during his junior and senior years, he maintained a minimal level of observance. Upon graduation and thinking more seriously about his path and the one not taken, he realized that he never seriously gave *Yiddishkeit* a chance. If he was going to reject Torah and *mitzvohs* he wanted to know what exactly he was rejecting.

His father had been a donor and supporter of Ohr HaTzadikim and Henry had heard very positive things about the staff, and in particular about one of the *Roshei Yeshiva,* Rabbi Noson Gendelman. Rabbi Gendelman was not only a Torah scholar, but a secular scholar as well—a published poet, noted intellectual and a dynamic speaker. After graduation Henry decided to come to Ohr HaTzadikim for the year. He also had applied to law schools and was accepted to Harvard. He deferred his entry. That year at Ohr HaTzadikim changed his life. At the end of the year, he asked for and received a very unusual second deferment to Harvard.

On his first day, the dorm manager, Rabbi Chaim Salzman, sat Henry down to hear the rules of the *Yeshiva.* Henry steeled himself for the usual long list of "don'ts."

"Rule number one," Rabbi Salzman intoned, "no girls in the dorms."

"Rule number two, no drugs."

"And rule number three, no *chillul Shabbos b'farhesia* (public desecration of *Shabbat*) while on campus. We don't want to make the observant students feel uncomfortable."

Rabbi Salzman stopped talking.

Expecting about fifty more pages of rules, Henry asked: "What about the other rules?"

"What other rules?

"What about coming to *davening* on time? A dress code? Behavior off campus?"

"No other rules," Rabbi Salzman responded.

"You mean that's it. Three rules?"

"Yup. Listen Henry, if we told you that you couldn't do this or couldn't do that, or you had to do this or that, when you went back home, would you continue keeping the rules?"

"No."

"Precisely. What's the point of giving you all sorts of rules if you won't internalize and live by them?"

And with that, Henry was introduced to the Ohr HaTzadikim theory of Jewish Education. It suited him perfectly.

Henry found that the *rebbeim* were consistently brilliant. He had a boatload of questions and the answers he was given astounded him. Instead of the rote learning he experienced in day school, *Gemara, Chumash* and *Halacha* were now intellectual challenges. In addition, there was a structured approach to Jewish Philosophy taught by former university Philosophy professors. He loved it. Many of the *rabbeim* at the *Yeshiva* remain a major influence on Henry's life and the life of his family until today, thirty years later.

After his second year at Ohr HaTzadikim, Henry got married and began his studies at Harvard Law School. I asked Henry if he was impressed by the professors at Harvard after spending two years at Ohr HaTzadikim. His answer was: "The professors I had at Harvard were outstanding, but never rose to the level of my *rebbeim* at Ohr HaTzadikim."

After graduating *magna cum laude* from Law School, Henry returned to Ohr HaTzadikim for another year—this time living off campus with his wife and their first two children. During that year, Henry began teaching what he had learned at the *Yeshiva* to English speaking students at Hebrew University. Today Henry is the Managing Partner at his family's law practice—The Robinson Law firm, a major East Coast injury firm. He and his wife, Chana, and family live in Northern New Jersey, where they are pillars of the Jewish community. Chana is the General Studies Principal of a *Bais Yaakov* there. Henry is still learning and speaks to Jewish audiences all over the world.

CHAPTER XI
The Sheva Mitzvohs Bnei Noach (The Seven Noahide Commandments)

There is another cohort of students, representing approximately ten percent of the *Yeshiva's* student population – *gerim* (converts*)*. Some of their stories are almost unbelievable.

But, before continuing with more stories about the fascinating people I met at the *Yeshiva*, an introduction to the *Seven Mitzvohs Bnei Noach* is necessary, since they are the entry point for many who eventually convert to Judaism.

Judaism is not a missionizing religion. In fact, it's not a religion at all. The word "Judaism" is a recent invention. While its origins are in the ancient Greek word *"Ioudaismos"*, that term did not imply religious beliefs, but rather "to side with or imitate the [Judeans]" *(see* ιουδαΐζειν. Liddell, Henry George; Scott, Robert; *An Intermediate Greek–English Lexicon* Oxford University Press 1843). Only in the 1400's did it enter the English language as a term describing the religion of the Jews. Because the word "Judaism" is not a Jewish invention, one will not find in the writings of our Rabbis and Sages over the ages a formulaic pledge of allegiance or doxology that defines the essence of "Jewishness."

Being Jewish means being a part of a huge family. The Jewish family began with Abraham. Adam and Eve weren't Jewish, nor were their sons and daughters or grandchildren.

Noah and his children weren't Jewish. It was only in the 20th generation after Adam and Eve that Abraham, the progenitor of the Jewish Family, was born. By that time people had abandoned the worship of one G-d and instead worshiped idols, whom, they believed, had power over every aspect of their lives.

We are used to thinking that idol worshipers were primitive, illogical, and intellectually challenged. But, as I've heard from my rabbis, their beliefs weren't silly or illogical. They weren't the result of primitive thinking born from fear of the dark and of evil forces. As anthropologists have discovered studying so-called "primitive cultures" that survive today, ancient man was not less intelligent than we are. The opposite is plausibly true.

As archeology has regularly discovered, ancient peoples were highly sophisticated, poetic, artistic, musical, scientific, and technically advanced within the confines of their materials. Their philosophy was based on empirical observations.

If a living being died a natural death, there must be a force in the world that caused that change in state from life to death to occur. A god of death, Satan, the Grim Reaper, the Hindu god Yama, or Mexican Santa Muerte must have that power over the life force. If one could propitiate that god, then the person offering the sacrifice might buy some more time on Earth. To concretize that philosophy, an idol representing death would be fashioned and offerings made to it. If a person who was afraid of death was saved, he might impute to that idol some magical power and it itself was revered as not just a representation of the god of death, but that the god dwelt inside the statue. Since flies' swarm around a dead carcass, people believed that flies were more powerful than death, since they live from death, or maybe were even born from death. That manifested itself in the belief in *Beelzebub*—(which is Hebrew for "lord of the flies").

In *Bereshis* (Genesis), the first book of the Bible, the action of washing the feet before entering the house is mentioned several times. Our commentaries explain that in those days people worshiped the dust on their feet. The phrase: "From dust you come and to dust you shall return," (Genesis 3:19) reflects that eternal and ubiquitous nature of dust. It's where we came from and what we will become. What could be more powerful than dust? It too became a god. Similar ideas extended to every other aspect of life. Abraham insisted on washing the feet before entering the house to show that dust is not supreme. It has no place or importance in his house.

Abraham, variously described as a child or middle-aged man, came to the realization that there was only one power in the world. One G-d. And that all aspects of life were ruled by Him. He might have angels to carry out missions, but they had no inherent powers. They functioned only as agents of the one G-d.

His children Ishmael (*Yishmael)* and Isaac (*Yitzchok*) followed in their father's beliefs. *Yitzchok* was chosen by G-d to be the leader of the incipient Jewish family in the next generation. Yitzchok was the father of Yaacov and Esav. Yaacov was chosen by G-d to be the leader of the family in that next generation. Yaacov had twelve sons. Those twelve sons became the leaders of tribes of Israel and their children went down to Egypt where they multiplied greatly and upon being taken out of Egyptian slavery became a Nation of many millions at Mt. Sinai, where we were given the Torah which contains 613 categories of commandments.

Had we not received the Torah we would have been

obligated to continue keeping only seven categories of commandments (the *Sheva Mitzvohs*). These were given to Noah when he left the Ark after the flood. And, as all humanity is descended from Noah, we were all obligated in them.

They are:
1. Not to worship idols.
2. Not to curse God.
3. Not to commit murder.
4. Not to commit adultery, bestiality, or sexual immorality.
5. Not to steal.
6. Not to eat flesh torn from a living animal.
7. To establish courts of justice.

Jews believe that anyone who is not born Jewish can be a perfectly righteous person by following these rules. They do not have to keep Shabbos and they can eat almost any food they like, including McDonald cheeseburgers at the beach on Saturday while playing the guitar. Well, maybe not McDonald's cheeseburgers.

The Problem with Cheeseburgers

Those familiar with the mechanics of the slaughterhouse know that cows are stunned by two common means. One is called the "captive bolt" and the other is electric shock. The first method shoots a bolt of metal into the skull of the animal. It might die immediately or might linger for a while until it dies from being eviscerated. In the case of stunning by electric shock, the cow is usually rendered unconscious and then bled and carved up. It is by no means certain that the animal is dead when his limbs are sawed off. It is highly likely that most meat sold in the world is cut from a live animal—a violation of prohibition number six. (I have, on occasion, told interested Christians, that they should only buy kosher meat to ensure that they are not violating one of the *Sheva Mitzvohs).*

Of the other six *mitzvohs* only the first presents a problem to followers of the Catholic or Orthodox Church. Even though Catholic theologians might argue that the images in their churches are just statuary representing the ideals of those depicted, I lived in Spain, and I have first-hand knowledge that many devout Catholics believe in the power of the actual statue.

So, if a non-Jew could live a righteous life by following the *Sheva Mitzvohs,* why would anyone choose to become Jewish? We have many thousands of laws and customs to keep. We need to pray three times a day for a total of approximately two hours. We can't eat lobster, shrimp, and bacon. Why do all this stuff when you don't have to? And why would the Jews accept such irrational people into our family?

The *Midrash* in *Shemos Rabbah, Parshas Yisro,* states that all the present and future souls of the Jewish People stood at Mount Sinai. The *gerim* are those souls that were temporarily lost and then found their way back to the family.

The Remingtons

When I first came to the *Yeshiva,* I met three Remington brothers from the Blue Ridge Mountains of Tennessee. These were full-blooded "mountain boys" whose ancestors had come to the American Colonies in the 17th and 18th centuries. They grew up in a wooden shack in a backwoods holler with no indoor plumbing, no electricity and no running water except for the stream about a hundred yards from their front door. Their neighbors were members of their extended family. And they could play old-time favorites like "Turkey in the Straw" on the fiddle, guitar, and harmonica like bluegrass professionals. There wasn't anything remotely Jewish about their dirty blond hair and beards and piercing blue eyes. They looked like the spitting image of "Johnny Reb" of Civil War mythology. Yet these guys were in Ohr HaTzadikim learning *Gemara*. And they were good at it. Not only that, but they could also *daven* for the congregation, sounding like they had been brought up in an Ashkenazi *yeshivish* home. Obviously, these guys had Jewish souls locked into *goyishe* bodies.

Their story is fascinating. Contrary to popular belief, these mountain people are not idiots or inbred imbeciles. They are as intelligent as you or me, or maybe even smarter. Their father was the pastor of their Baptist church. Its members were all relatives. Being of an intellectual bent, the pastor made a critical reading of the Bible. He couldn't understand why he and his flock didn't follow a literal reading of the words. They kept most of the Ten Commandments, as they understood them, but even though they were Protestant Evangelicals, they had a cross on top of the church. It seemed to their father that the cross smacked of an image. The third commandment in his Bible stated: "Thou shalt not make unto thee any graven image."

Pastor Remington knew that the Bible was originally written in Hebrew, but he couldn't read Hebrew. And to really understand the Ten Commandments he thought he should ask someone that did. He drove to Memphis to search for a rabbi to help him. The city phone book had a few listings for rabbis. The first one he called was a Reform one. Pastor Remington knew nothing about different communities of Jews, but he knew his Bible. In speaking to the Reform rabbi, he immediately discovered that the rabbi was an ignoramus. He didn't even know the relevant Biblical passages. The Reform rabbi suggested that he speak to Rabbi Cohen, the only Orthodox rabbi in town, who owned the Jewish bookstore. Rabbi Cohen was also the son-in-law of Rabbi Nissin Holderman, a senior rabbi at Ohr HaTzadikim in Jerusalem.

The relationship between the Pastor and the Rabbi flourished. Rabbi Cohen urged the Pastor to keep the *Sheva Mitzvohs Bnei Noach* and to encourage his family and flock to do the same. At next Sunday's sermon, Pastor Remington announced that he was taking down the cross on top of the church because it violated the Third Commandment. This caused a gigantic furor among the congregation. Half the flock agreed with the Pastor and half didn't. And since they were all family, it created a rupture in the fabric of the family as well. While guns weren't used to fight the feud, an atmosphere of Hatfields and McCoys pervaded the holler. A few months after that initial meeting, Rabbi Cohen was asked by a synagogue in Atlanta, Georgia to become its spiritual leader. Pastor Remington and his boys, now observing the *Sheva Mitzvohs*, would get up early on Saturday mornings and drive five hours down to Atlanta to hear the Rabbi's speech. After about a year, the older boys decided that they wanted more. They wanted to convert. They were excellent students and mastered the material required for conversion and then set out for Ohr HaTzadikim in Jerusalem. Their younger siblings and mother soon followed. Their father, the Pastor, after living as a Noahide for many years, also made the transition to conversion. The eleven siblings and their parents all eventually settled in Israel. Some of them became great scholars and are now *rebbes* and *roshei yeshiva*. Some have supported themselves and their families by cabinetmaking—a skill they learned back in the Blue Ridge Mountains of Tennessee.

Binyamin Hammond

Binyamin's story could be titled "Out of Africa." And that would be appropriate, because we too, on the holiday of Passover, celebrate our own "out of Africa" story. But his is slightly different.

Binyamin grew up in a staunchly Christian home in Port Harcourt, Nigeria. He's the oldest of three children. His father, Samuel Hammond, was a very popular Pentecostal minister. The church that he founded would regularly draw over 1,000 people on a Sunday.

In 2003 and 2004 his father attended a Christian conference held in South Africa. While there, he felt a calling to move to South Africa and open a church. After establishing his church in Roodepoort, a suburb west of Johannesburg, he sent for his family. Soon he was drawing large crowds of 500-600 people a week and opened a branch in Soweto, a large Black township nearby, where he was also very successful. He had also opened branches in Ghana and in a number of cities in the United States.

In 2011, Samuel had a dream. In it he was wrestling with a man who kept yelling at him, "It's time for Israel. Think Israel." Until that point, Israel and the Jews had not been topics of discussion in the church or in the Hammond household, but that dream changed his perspective. A few weeks later he began to introduce the idea of supporting Israel into his sermons. He organized rallies in support of Israel and began to bring groups of Africans to Israel. He also started an organization called "Africa-Israel Initiative." The Israeli government took note of his support and sent representatives to his rallies. The South African Zionist organization also invited his father to speak at their plenums. Binyamin, still in his teens, was the Vice President of the Youth Division of the organization.

On one of his return flights from Israel, Binyamin's father noticed an Orthodox Jewish man reading an English titled religious book. He asked him what the book was about and where he might get a copy. The book was a popular Breslov title, "The Garden of Faith." The man told him the name of a bookstore in Johannesburg that carried it. His father bought it, read it, and returned to the store to buy many more books. He discussed what he read with his wife and with Binyamin. He was beginning to see the truth of Judaism and started moving away from Christian ideology. Binyamin, alongside his siblings, were all drawn to this new pool of wisdom.

His father slowly started introducing changes in the church. His sermons were now primarily about the need to support Israel and the Jews as the "priests to the nations." This emphasis on Jews and Israel irritated many members and they dropped out of the church. As his world started crumbling before him, Binyamin felt the need to get clarity as to his own beliefs. He began a serious study of the history of Christianity.

At about the same time, his father instructed Binyamin, who was also the church's music director, to substitute the name of G-d for that of the Christian deity in all the songs and hymns that were sung at the services. This created another huge rift in the church.

Changes were also afoot at home. One of his father's Jewish friends invited the Hammond family to come to his home for Shabbos. Binyamin and his father went to *shul* on Friday night for the first time. It was an extremely emotional and spiritual experience for both. The structure of the prayers, the silent *Shemoneh Esrei prayer*, the tunes, and the Shabbos atmosphere were intoxicating. The delicious meal that followed with its *zemiros* (songs of praise) and *divrei Torah* (Torah explanations) were nothing like they ever experienced. The whole family was touched beyond words.

Soon afterwards, the Hammond family started to observe Shabbos and *kashrus* to the best of their understanding. That meant not leaving home on the Sabbath, having family meals, and not watching TV. Their knowledge of keeping kosher came from the Written Law. Not living in a Jewish community, they weren't aware at first of kosher butcher shops, and so armed with a book on kosher slaughtering, Binyamin and his father went out to farms, bought animals, and *shechted* (slaughtered) them for food. Not being used to killing animals, that exercise was short-lived. As a result, the family switched to eating a lot of fish.

Now the Hammond family was forced to live a double life—closet "Jew-ish" people for six days a week, and church leaders on Sunday. They lived like this for over a year, but it couldn't last. One Sunday, his father, in the middle of his sermon, announced that he and his family had decided to convert to Judaism, and that he was disbanding the church. He urged those who wished to stay close to him to become Noahides. His church would now be a Noahide worship center. He would still be their spiritual leader. The *Beis Din* in Johannesburg was convinced of the family's sincerity. After two years of study, they all converted and moved to Glenhazel, a Jewish enclave in Johannesburg. In 2020 the whole family made *Aliyah* and now lives in Israel. They discovered that if one is truly devoted to attaching oneself to G-d and experiencing the beauty of Jewish Family life, one will want to do more, and not be satisfied with just the seven *mitzvohs* of Noah.

Yosef Hamadou

Yosef Hamadou from Mbanga, Cameroon, a small town about 50 miles from Douala, the country's largest city, was the scion of a distinguished clan in the Bamileké Tribe of Bangangté in West Cameroon. His grew up in his grandmother's house. His great-grandfather, *Men MaFeun Nga'an* (the title "Men MaFeun" literally means "son of the king's mother", or "prince"), had been a ruler in the region and his grandmother was the matriarch of the family. The family was devoutly Catholic, and Yosef was an altar boy at the Cathedral in Douala, where he lived with his uncle while attending high school. He later moved to Singapore, where he lived with his aunt and uncle for post high school studies and then to Sydney, Australia where he became an Accountant and Financial Planner.

His office in Sydney was in a building owned by three brothers. Yosef was still a very religious Christian although he had switched his affiliation to a Protestant church. Every afternoon Yosef would set aside time to pray and read his Bible. One day, one of the landlords came into his office, saw him studying, and asked what he was reading. Yosef told him. In the course of conversation, the landlord mentioned that he and his family were Jews.

Yosef was amazed. Until then he had never met a Jew. To Yosef, Jews were a mythical people who lived thousands of years ago. As a boy he had been taught in his catechism classes that because the Jews had killed the messiah and rejected him as their savior, they were cursed throughout history and brought strife and misery wherever they went. And because of this rejection, the Jews were replaced by the Christians who had now become the "new Jews." He had no idea that Jews practiced their religion currently or that there were communities of them anywhere in the world except for a country named Israel, which was causing problems for the Middle East and the world. But that country also seemed rather mysterious and mythical to him. And yet here and now in Sydney, there was a living, breathing Jew in his very office.

Yosef had many unresolved questions about religion. The preacher in his church in Sydney couldn't or wouldn't answer them—telling Yosef to trust in Jesus and his questions would be answered. He tried, but the questions remained. He met the other brothers and had deep conversations about religion with them and especially the oldest brother, Hymie, who looked to Yosef like the image of a Biblical patriarch. He had a long beard, a head covering, and strings coming out of his belt. The answers he gave to Yosef's questions about the "Old Testament" were eye opening. Yosef had never heard such logical and well thought out responses. But, when it came to his questions about the "New Testament," Hymie had no answers, as he never read it. But he knew someone who did. Hymie told Yosef about a friend of his whom he thought Yosef would like to meet.

Rabbi Eli Cohen is the rabbi of a *shul* in the Sydney suburb of Newtown and the head of an organization called "Jews for

Judaism". Its goal is to save those Jews who are targeted by Christian missionaries. Its method includes pointing out the inconsistencies in Christian thought and outright mistranslation or fabrications of Torah texts. Rabbi Cohen was extremely well versed in Christian texts and theology, and eminently qualified to answer all of Yosef's questions. Probably the most impressive quality that Yosef observed about him was the rabbi's willingness to admit to not knowing an answer, and then getting back to him with the answer after researching it. In his experience, no Christian priest or pastor had admitted to not knowing an answer to a question about religion.

After several meetings, Rabbi Cohen invited Yosef to attend his synagogue. He loved it. Rabbi Cohen suggested that Yosef keep the *Sheva mitzvos*. Yosef accepted this obligation and observed those commandments, but after a few months he felt it wasn't enough. He thirsted for a closer connection to G-d and the Torah. Rabbi Cohen tried to dissuade him from converting, but after months of persisting, Rabbi Cohen finally introduced Yosef to Rabbi Jeremy Lawrence, the Rabbi of the Great Synagogue of Sydney. Rabbi Lawrence recommended Yosef to the *Beis Din* of Sydney, which agreed to supervise his study and eventual conversion. Immediately upon his conversion, after wrapping up his affairs in Sydney, he came to the *Yeshiva* where he studied for a few years before getting married and entering the workforce as a devout *Jew*.

Rabbi Natan Gamedze

Rabbi Natan Gamedze, a prince of the Royal House of Swaziland came to the *Yeshiva* shortly after graduating from

Oxford with a degree in Linguistics. A brilliant young man, who was already fluent in 11 languages, he had become interested in Hebrew Language while at Oxford and soon mastered it. Delving into the texts of the *Rambam* (Maimonidies), he was so taken with the ideas and laws expressed therein that he began teaching the texts to Jewish students at Oxford. Upon graduation, Hebrew University in Jerusalem offered him a full scholarship to do a PhD in Hebrew Language and Literature. Natan skipped the step of the *Sheva Mitzvohs*. He knew in his soul that he needed to rejoin his Jewish family. He found his way to the *Yeshiva* and learnt here for five years, while earning his PhD. He later received *smicha* (ordination) from the rabbis of one of the most elite *yeshivos* in the world. He now learns and teaches Torah in Israel.

Binyamin Liao

The ancient Chinese philosophers wrote extensively about the ideal way of life. Values of respect for elders, compassion, reverence, humaneness, decency, righteousness, and altruism run deep in Chinese culture. Mao Tse-Tung, following the success of his communist revolution in 1949, sought to uproot the traditions of the past, which he felt were impediments to the implementation of his vision for a materialistic society. His war on the Chinese past reached its climax in the Cultural Revolution in the 1960s. He did an effective job. By the time Binyamin Liao was born in the 1970s, ancient Chinese wisdom had been all but erased, and a new religion of utilitarianism replaced it. Whatever worked was "good" and what didn't work was "bad." In this philosophy Binyamin grew up.

His parents, though, thought differently. Even as a young boy he was made to understand that there was a righteous way to live, and he was expected to find that way. His mother, a highly educated woman, taught him to read the ancient Chinese symbols and to decipher the teachings of Lao Tzu. He gained a deep level of understanding of the ancient wisdom, but while it was poetic and beautiful, it was difficult to know how to apply it to specific situations. Without a teacher the individual was left unguided and had to find his own path in life. And in post Mao's China, a teacher of the "old" philosophy was in danger of imprisonment or death.

School and work did not foster independent or unconventional thought. Binyamin studied hard and eventually graduated from an elite University with a master's degree in electrical engineering. He worked in a government funded, cutting edge, hi-tech business and was very good at what he did, but he was still bothered by questions: "Why am I here on this earth? What are my life's goals? Am I here just to make computers less vulnerable to hackers; to make a better machine? Is that all there is to life?" Another question that he pondered endlessly was: "How does a righteous person act in a given situation?"

This last question was illustrated in stark relief one day when he was buying some fruit in the market. He asked the seller politely to give him a sample to taste. For some unexplained reason, the seller flew into a rage, berating Binyamin, and flung a piece of the fruit at Binyamin's head. Binyamin didn't know how a righteous person should react. Should he shout back? Should he also throw a piece of fruit at the man? He stayed silent but was confused. What was the proper response?

He was working in network security in Shanghai when a friend suggested that he apply for a work visa for Australia. Although he really didn't have a great desire to leave China, he applied anyway. About a year later he received a letter from the Australian Government telling him that his application was accepted.

Although he spoke virtually no English, Binyamin moved to Melbourne. As he would say now, "*mishaneh makom, mishaneh mazal*" (changing location changes one's luck). At first it didn't look like that. Because he didn't have the language skills, he couldn't find a job. He spent almost his first two years in Australia just learning English. Finally, with his savings almost exhausted, he got a job in IT with the Melbourne City Council. He later moved to Sydney where he found work in IT with the Forestry Commission of New South Wales.

As the years passed, those eternal questions took on greater and greater urgency. One day a co-worker in his office gave him a book to read. It was the Bible. He had never seen one before. The first part of the book fascinated him. It was called the Old Testament. He read it and felt intuitively that it was not authored by a human, and that it contained ultimate truths. When he was asked by the lender what he thought, Binyamin told him that the first part of the Book was amazing and true. As to the second part, the so-called New Testament, he was not impressed. Binyamin asked the man if he also believed that the Bible was the word of G-d. The man answered affirmatively. Why then didn't he keep *Shabbat* and wear *tzitzit*, keep k*osher* and do all the numerous other laws contained therein? The man answered that he wasn't required to because his savior had absolved him from those obligations. This struck Binyamin as absurd, and he just kept re-reading and studying the first part of the book—The Five Books of Moses.

Up to this point Binyamin hadn't knowingly ever met a Jew. One day, an electrician came to his office to repair some of the wiring. He had a cloth head covering, and some strings sticking out of his pants. Binyamin was curious. He asked the electrician the meaning of those things he was wearing. At first the man avoided a direct answer. Upon repeated questioning, he revealed that he was an Orthodox Jew, and that these were articles of clothing that we wear—a *kippa and tzitzit*. Binyamin had many questions about them and other things that he had read about in the *Chumash*. The electrician didn't have many answers, but referred him, instead, to his rabbi. Binyamin met the rabbi, who saw his serious interest in becoming a member of the Jewish People, and he, in turn, referred Binyamin to the *Beis Din* of Sydney, which supervises conversions. Binyamin was an eager and serious learner and completed the requirements of the *Beis Din* in fifteen months and converted.

The next five years were spent working and getting more deeply involved in learning Torah. He read extensively but had not yet mastered the texts in the original Hebrew. He decided that the only way he could make the progress that he desired was to learn in *yeshiva*. He had met a rabbi from Ohr HaTzadikim at the Adas *shul i*n Sydney and decided that Ohr HaTzadikim in Jerusalem was where he needed to be. In January 2018 he made *Aliyah* and joined the *yeshiva,* where he studied for another two years and eventually married another Chinese convert. I attended their wedding in the Old City of Jerusalem.

I questioned Binyamin about the incident in the marketplace in China. Now that he's Jewish and has learned and read extensively, how would he now react to the seller who threw that piece of food at him? Without any hesitation, Binyamin answered with a quote from the Rabbis: "To be silent in the face of insult and disparagement—I would cherish that moment as one of the happiest of my life."

Wally McGuire

Another student, Wally, represents a segment of our student population who grew up as Christians and later discovered that they were Jewish. I have met a surprising number of Jews like Wally in the last thirty years. Many of them are children or grandchildren of Holocaust survivors who hid their Jewish identities from their children to protect them from the tragedies and traumas that they experienced in Europe.

Wally was born to a Jewish mother and Catholic father in Chattanooga, Tennessee. His mother, the daughter of Austrian Jews, who were on one of the last boats out of Europe before WWII, was born in Brooklyn, but moved to Biloxi, Mississippi with her divorced mother as a very young girl. Her mother, Wally's grandmother, was not involved with a Jewish community and had almost no contact with her family in Brooklyn. Wally's mother moved to Memphis, Tennessee for college and married his father, a non-Jewish accountant. She never mentioned to Wally and his siblings the fact that she was born into a Jewish family.

Shortly after Wally was born the family moved to a small town near Gatlinburg, in Eastern Tennessee, where his father opened an accounting office. As is true with many small towns in the South and Appalachia, Gatlinburg is a stronghold of the Pentecostal Church, one of larger groups in Evangelical

Christianity. There are different types of Pentecostal Churches. The more extreme ones are the "snake handlers". During their Sunday prayers, they pick up poisonous rattlesnakes, copperheads, and cottonmouths from their enclosure at the front of the church, as a proof of their faith. Many are bitten and die. Among the more moderate Pentecostal Churches, like the one that Wally and his family belonged to, belief manifests itself by "speaking in tongues," "laying hands on the sick," and "casting out devils."

When they "speak in tongues", the worshiper falls to the ground in a kind epileptic fit, and babbles unintelligible words or syllables (glossolalia) which are then "translated" or "interpreted" by the pastor; or the pastor himself can be seized by "the spirit" and babble away and then coming back to his senses will explain his "prophetic experience."

Wally went to a Pentecostal school where "speaking in tongues" was also a common occurrence. In the middle of a math or English class, the teacher would fall to the ground and babble incoherently and after a few minutes would come back to his senses and accuse this boy or that of certain sinful behavior that had been "revealed" to him. Boys would also fall to the ground and speak in tongues and the teacher would "translate" their words as naming one of the other boys in the class as a miscreant.

When Wally was eight, he first met his mother's aunt at his sister's wedding in Chicago. His great aunt, a European-born religious Jew, lived in Brooklyn, NY. She revealed to Wally that he was Jewish. It made such an impression on him that to this day he remembers her very next words. "Every year at the Passover Seder we say, 'Next Year in Jerusalem.' That (hope) is what got our family out of Czarist Russia to Poland and after pogroms in Poland to Austria and then to America. This is your community. You can accept it or not, but you should know that this is your community."

Thereafter, because of those words, knowing that he was different, he never again felt comfortable in the Pentecostal Church or in his Pentecostal school. Anti-Semitism was also rampant in the small town of Wally's youth. Almost everyone there believed that a "Deep State" was running the country and that its manipulators were the Jews. He kept his Jewishness a secret.

After graduation from high school, Wally was eager to leave Tennessee. He was the only student in his high school class to do so. He went to a Christian college in a Norfolk, Virginia. He deliberately chose a Christian school, so that his family couldn't object to him going there. Now that he was out of state, he felt free of his small town "claustrophobia" and was ready to explore the wider world. The college followed a more moderate and inclusive Protestant doctrine, and it was located near a Jewish community. Wally was planning to unearth the meaning of his heritage.

When he was nineteen, he had his first exposure to Judaism at a Chabad House in nearby Norfolk, Virginia. He kept going back and became a regular there. Wally graduated college in 2016 and was accepted to the graduate school at Yale where he finished a year of study toward a master's degree in Geopolitics of the Middle East and Islamic Political Philosophy.

After his first year in New Haven, his rabbi suggested that Wally come to Israel on an Orthodox Union Birthright trip and encouraged him to check out *yeshivot*. He didn't need much convincing. He came in May and was very moved. He took a leave of absence from Yale and studied for a year at Ohr

HaTzadikim. Feeling a strong attachment to the Land and the People of Israel, he made *Aliyah*, volunteered for a combat unit in the IDF and is planning to get married soon. He hopes to finish his degree at Hebrew University after his Army service and to eventually find employment in Israel's Foreign Ministry.

Akiva Pearlman

There is an apocryphal story about a young Jewish man who in his spiritual quest had traveled the world, worshiping in Native American sweat lodges, taking *ayahuasca* in the jungles of the Amazon under the guidance of a native *shaman,* experiencing a Catholic Mass at the Vatican, bowing on a prayer mat in Mecca and eventually reaching a mountain peak in the Himalayas where he met a famous Buddhist *guru*. In answer to the traveler's question as to the meaning of life and what his path through it should be, the *guru*, who was alternatively an old Jew from Brooklyn or the *Dali Lama*, answered with a question: "Who are you, my son?" "A Jew from New York," answered the traveler. "Then what are you doing here? You should investigate your own traditions. Go to *yeshiva* in Israel." He did, ending up in Ohr HaTzadikim and eventually becoming a great *talmid chacham*. This is not Akiva's story. It's nothing compared to his.

Akiva was raised in Chelmsford, Massachusetts, after his family moved there from Seattle when he was two years old. They were a very secular family, and he grew up without knowledge of *Shabbos, Rosh Hashanah* or even *Yom Kippur*. They did try Chanukah for a couple of years but reverted to Xmas the next. One might say, they couldn't see the forest for the Tree. But they knew they were Jews and were proud of it, although Akiva and his siblings had no idea what it meant to be Jewish.

Akiva was a very curious, artistic, and precocious child. He loved reading, science, and mathematics. When he was ten years old, his aunt gave him a camera as a birthday present. It was wrapped in a newspaper from Japan. He was as excited about the newspaper as he was about the camera. The mysterious and seemingly unintelligible characters fascinated him. He announced to his mother that one day he was going to be able to read that newspaper.

By the end of high school, he wasn't sure what he wanted to study. His mother suggested that since he could draw so well, he should study art. Akiva received a full scholarship to study art at the University of Massachusetts at Amherst. Professor Wong, a well-known Chinese artist, taught one of his first art classes. Akiva loved the professor, who peppered his lectures with Chinese philosophy. After criticizing one of Akiva's paintings, he said to him: "Not everyone can be a good artist, you know." Taking the criticism to heart, Akiva dropped his major and switched to the study of Chinese language

He was a fast learner, but after two-and-a-half semesters of Chinese he felt the tug of the sciences and decided to drop out of the University to study Chinese medicine. With almost no money in his pocket, he hitchhiked to the West Coast, where he hoped to save up enough money for a one-way ticket to Taiwan. In those days Mainland China was closed to foreigners. He eventually got to Taiwan and began studying the Chinese language in earnest with the purpose of entering a Chinese medical school or getting an apprenticeship with a Chinese doctor.

Ever the perfectionist, Akiva insisted on mastering Mandarin so that he could speak without an accent. His language teacher told him that this was impossible. There were no foreigners who could master the tonal subtleties of the Chinese language. He would always sound like a foreigner. However, instead of discouraging him, it only made him try harder. He spent weeks mastering the pronunciation of two words that initially sounded the same to him. He then returned to the teacher, who told him that she couldn't believe what he had accomplished. After a few years his Chinese was impeccable. (I can attest to this fact, because I have been to kosher Chinese restaurants in New York with Akiva, and the owners have told me that they are astounded at how he speaks Mandarin perfectly and without an accent). In addition to studying Chinese, Akiva also studied art, music, and *Kung Fu*—Chinese martial arts.

One day he heard about a renowned Chinese doctor who was located at the base of a mountain in Central Taiwan. The doctor accepted him as an apprentice. Soon after beginning his training, Akiva heard that at the top of the mountain was a Buddhist monastery headed by an even more renowned master Chinese healer and Kung Fu expert, a true *shifu* (master teacher). Akiva went up the mountain and asked the master if he could learn Chinese medicine from him. The master told him that he could, but he would have to follow all the rules of the monastery. Akiva agreed, with the proviso that he wouldn't have to become a Buddhist monk.

The monk's day began two hours before sunrise. Upon waking, the monk was required to drink 14 large bowls of water. This was followed by an hour of strenuous exercise and difficult pushups. When he arrived, Akiva could do 19 pushups.

All the other monks were doing hundreds. The master told him to add one pushup a day. (By the end of his stay he was doing 685 pushups without a break.) After bathing in a nearby freezing mountain spring, the monks would have a large breakfast and then tend to the daily chores, such as vegetable gardening and carrying huge buckets of water on their backs from the mountain spring to irrigate the monastery's gardens at the foot of the mountain.

Lunch was a bowl of rice and a bowl of water. A midday break was devoted to Buddhist study, including Kung Fu, Meditation, and calligraphy. The monks also made excursions into town to help the sick and needy. Bedtime was at nightfall. After many months of this regimen, Akiva began to question whether the master would ever teach him Chinese medicine. Whenever he asked to begin, the master put him off. Akiva knew he was being tested but didn't know why. He didn't want to wait forever.

After three years at the monastery, Akiva left. He had waited long enough. He was twenty-three years old and restless. He consulted with a few Chinese wise men as to his future and they all told him he should return to the States and get his undergraduate degree. He did. He completed his missing three years of college in one year, with a 4.0 average, and graduated with a degree in Chinese. Upon graduation he returned to China and began working as an English teacher to support his medical studies. After a "chance" meeting with a famous Chinese Kung Fu movie director, he was hired to play a major part in a new movie. The director also hired him to tutor the star of the film in the English language. During the lessons, the actor discovered that Akiva knew martial arts. Many of the Kung Fu movies at the time had a white American Kung Fu master as its antagonist. With his command of Chinese and martial arts, Akiva was a cinch to play the bad guy in the movies.

After a successful, but relatively brief acting career, Akiva moved to Japan, where he again pursued his desire to learn Chinese medicine. He mastered Japanese in a year but failed to find the right school in which to learn medicine.

Around this time Akiva's father passed away and he began to earnestly contemplate the meaning of life. Until then, although a Buddhist monk, he was an atheist. But he also had a sense that there was something much deeper going on in the world than the phenomena that met the eye. He threw himself into the teachings that he had previously learned only superficially as a monk. He examined Christian scriptures as well. Nothing satisfied him. There were too many unanswered questions and contradictions. He made a trip back to Boston to visit his mother and sent himself three large boxes of Jewish books from the local Jewish bookstore in Brookline. Back in Japan he pored through these books. One of them mentioned the idea from the *Sefer HaChinuch* that if someone is constantly involved in the performance of *mitzvos*, eventually he will come to believe in G-d. Akiva, always up for a challenge, decided to test this idea. He would keep the *mitzvos* (as he understood them from his reading) for a year and see what would happen. It worked! In less than six months of keeping *Shabbat* and *kashrut* and praying three times a day, he realized that there was a G-d who created the world and sustains it and who commanded the Jewish People to keep the *mitzvos*. He now knew what he must do. He came to Ohr HaTzadikim *Yeshiva* in Jerusalem. That's when I met Akiva.

After learning in the *Yeshiva* for three years, he moved to New York to find his *zivug* (wife). He met her after a long and grueling eight-year search. At the behest of a large U.S. *kashrut* organization, the couple moved to Shanghai, where Akiva set up their China office. Several years later, a large Israeli Real Estate development company asked Akiva to become its Chief Operating Office in its Beijing branch. In 2018, after fourteen years in China, and three children, the family moved from Beijing to Cleveland, Ohio, where Akiva is today employed as the COO of a large Midwestern real estate concern and a staunch member of its Orthodox Jewish Community.

I can honestly say that after more than thirty years at the *Yeshiva* I am as impressed with the quality of the staff and students as I was when I first came. But because I now know the staff much more intimately than I did then, I am even more impressed with them than before. It is an amazing testament to a school that fosters such devotion and loyalty from its staff and attracts and educates such outstanding students.

CHAPTER XII
Language

My struggles with the Hebrew language persist until today, over thirty-five years since I made *Aliyah*. I am still not quite as fluent in Hebrew as I am in Spanish. I often must ask someone addressing me to repeat what they said a second or third time until I understand. Since I sometimes must do this with English speakers, I could partly attribute this to old age hearing issues. But with Hebrew speakers it's more frequent. My reading and writing skills are better, but it is still a challenge for me to read Modern Hebrew books, newspapers, or magazines.

Of course, my coming to Israel was not exactly like the "greener" experience of my grandparents and great-grandparents when they came to America. I came with a better secular education and more money than most Israelis my age. Americans in Israel have, at least in some circles, an elite status. There are about one million Israelis who have left Israel and moved to the States, either as legal or illegal immigrants. America is a dream to them. They still think "the streets of America are paved with gold". For some of them that's true. So, when an American moves to Israel he's seen as someone who has either achieved his dream of materiality and now wishes to come back to the Homeland to "live the life of Goldberg" (like the "life of Riley"—but in a Jewish way), or his family is rich enough to support him.

I studied hard in the *Yeshiva* for the first five years.

Thankfully, the payout from my old law firm was enough to support us without having to work, but then I needed to make a living, so I took the bar exam in Israel.

Because I had over five years of legal practice in America, I was able to take a lighter version of the bar exam—the written part. Because Israeli law is based, in part, on English Common Law, a lawyer coming from a Common Law country, like the USA, U.K or Australia, has an advantage over those coming from countries with other legal systems. Those lawyers, who come to Israel with less than five years of practice, must also stand for oral exams, which are reputed to be more difficult than the written ones. I only had to learn all Israeli law and write exams on nine or ten different areas of it. Although the test was in Hebrew, we were allowed to write the answers in English. I took a bar review course and within two months of starting the course I had passed all the exams and was ready to begin my requisite *"staje"*—my internship. I did it with an American, Arnold Susskind, originally from Miami Beach, who had gone to Yeshiva University and then Harvard Law School. I can honestly say I didn't learn too much. Most of his clients were English speakers and much of his practice was also in English. But I gained a passing familiarity with the workings of the Israeli legal system and especially the Land recording system, which is quite complicated when compared to real estate practice in the States. And I also got to learn Talmud with a brilliant *gemara* student (Arnold), when we had free time.

CHAPTER XIII
Education of Children

It is, of course, incumbent on every parent to provide for the proper education of his children. And just as no two children are alike, except perhaps for identical twins, each child's needs and talents must be considered before choosing their proper school. As that wisest of men, *Shlomo HaMelech* (King Solomon) said: "Educate the child according to his path…" (Proverbs 22:6).

When we lived in Cleveland our choices were limited. When our oldest, Miriam, was ready for kindergarten there was only one religious' school—The Hebrew Academy of Cleveland. When our second daughter was of age a second school, with a more *yeshivish* student population had opened, and we sent Rochi there. In Israel the choices were seemingly limitless. I would like to say that we did extensive research into each school, weighing the academic standards, the type of parent likely to send to that school, the reputation of the principal and staff, the quality of the teachers, and behavior of the student population. But that wouldn't be true. We sent our girls where everyone else in our neighborhood sent theirs.

We enrolled Miriam into the 4th grade class at the *Bais Yaacov* of *Sanhedria Murchevet* and Rochi was enrolled in a *gan chova* (Kindergarten) in the nearby Bucharian neighborhood. Miriam, who was nine when the school year began, took public transportation. I walked Rochi to school and picked her up at 1:15pm.

Both girls had trouble with the language at first, but after six months they sounded to me like natives.

Miriam had a difficult time socially. The girls in her class had designated her as the *"Americana"*. The funny thing was that many of those girls came from homes with at least one American parent. In the Ashkenazi *charedie* society of Israel, to be an American is not a positive thing. Americans are looked down upon as generally less religious. Even learning English was, at the time, frowned upon. It indicated that you were a part of the world that was "modern", and which intruded on "real" Jewish values. The whole American culture, from sports to movies to free thinking and *laissez faire* morality was something that children needed to be protected from. Learning English was, therefore, like learning the Devil's own language. While Miriam wasn't shunned, she wasn't part of the "in crowd" at school either. It is, of course, entirely possible that even if she had been born in Israel, she would have suffered the same fate. Her father is a *baal teshuva* and her mother a convert—neither fitting to enter the purity of the upper echelons of *charedie* society.

Unfortunately, this stigma followed Miriam throughout her school career in the *Bais Yaacov* system. It came to a head when she was ready to enter high school.

The Israeli religious educational system is not like that in the States. The reason is that the First Amendment of the American Constitution forbids public funding of religious schools. The State of Israel, a Jewish country, funds public schools that are either religious or non-religious. There are also private schools, both religious and non-religious, which receive partial State funding. The State sponsored religious public schools are called *Mamlachti Dati* schools. They are very

Zionistic and modern (meaning laxer in observance) than the *charedie* schools. Most of those schools are coed. The *Chinuch Atzmai* (Independent Education) schools are *charedie* and publicly supported in Jerusalem, which has a majority religious population. The girls' schools are called *Bais Yaacov* and the boys' schools have no specific name. They do not share the same buildings.

High schools are competitive. The better ones are very selective. When Miriam was in eighth grade and applying to high school she wanted to go to the *"Beis Yaacov haChadash"* (the "New *Bais Yaacov"*). It was where many of her friends were going and was academically the most demanding of the *Beis Yaacov* High Schools. She applied in November for the following year. Miriam was an excellent student, very well-mannered and *tznius* (modest). There was no good reason why she shouldn't have been accepted. Interviews began at the end of January. She told me that many of the girls in her class had been called for interviews, but she hadn't been. I called the *Chadash* and asked why she hadn't been given an interview. The secretary told me that they hadn't reached her name yet. But "don't worry, she'll be called." At the end of February, she still hadn't been called. I called again. "Don't worry we'll be calling her soon." A couple of months later, near *Pesach* (Passover) time, she still hadn't been called. We were getting quite nervous.

I called again. This time I spoke to the *saganit* (vice principal), who ran the school. "Don't worry we'll be in touch right after *Pesach*." They weren't. I called again. "I'm so sorry, but the classes are filled, we have no more space."

"But that's not fair," I said. "She never even had an interview."

"I'm sorry, but that's the situation."

At this point I turned to Reb Shraga Weinstein, one of the *Roshei Yeshiva* of Ohr HaTzadikim with my problem. Someone had told me that Reb Shraga had been one of the founders of the school and that he had *protekzia* (influence) there.

I laid out the problem. He asked me why I hadn't come to him sooner. I told him that I had only recently found out that he was a founder of the school and that even had I known, my daughter was a model student and there was no reason for me to think that she wouldn't get into her first choice.

Reb Shraga shook his head.

"Don't you know how things work here?" he said.

"It has nothing to do with what you know, but who you know."

This is called in Hebrew "*protekzia.*"

He could have just let it go at that and I would have learned an important lesson of life in Israel. But he didn't let it go. He told me not to worry, that he'd get my daughter into the school.

The first thing he did was to arrange an interview with the Vice Principal. I was to accompany Miriam to the interview. My wife, who is ideologically opposed to using *protekzia,* or any privilege, wanted no part of it. I assumed they would ask me what I do for a living. In America when answering that question, I would of course say I was a lawyer. After all, an attorney is a prestigious profession. But I was also a *rebbe* at Ohr HaTzadikim and didn't know if I should mention both professions, or only one—*Orach Din* (lawyer).

Reb Shraga jumped.

"Whatever you do, don't say you're a lawyer."

"Just say you're a *rebbe.*"

Until then I had no idea how professionals were looked

down upon by the *charedie* society in Israel. That certainly wasn't the case in America. Being a lawyer in Cleveland was prestigious in the *frum* community. Here, however, it meant that you spent several years studying in a co-ed University and mixing with non-religious men and women—definitely a negative. It then occurred to me that in all the years that I had been *davening* with a *Yerushalmi* minyan in a nearby neighborhood, I had never mentioned to anyone there that I was a lawyer. Now, I would positively avoid telling them that.

I don't know if vice principals are part of a secret society, but this one absolutely reminded me of Mrs. Rioux, the terror provoking vice-principal of my Junior High School. It was obvious that the *Saganit* had no interest in letting my daughter into the school and was only interviewing us because Reb Shraga had forced her hand. But she wasn't going to let it go further than the interview. I told her I was a *rebbe* and had learned in Telshe Yeshiva in Cleveland before moving to Israel and had been learning and teaching since I arrived. Miriam was well behaved and answered the perfunctory questions that were asked.

"We'll get back to you later. As I told you previously, the classes are all filled, but if something opens, we'll let you know."

As they say in Yiddish. "*A Nechtaga Tag!*" (Loosely translated as: "Good luck, Charlie!")

As September rolled around and the new school year was beginning, Miriam was now desperate. She could go the "*Yashan*", the "Old" *Bais Yaacov,* a school with thousands of girls which had a reputation for lower academic standards. It was also the preferred school for *Chassidishe* girls who would be getting married soon after high school and were not really interested in education.

Reb Shraga told me not to worry.

"But school starts next week." I told Reb Shraga.

"Don't worry, I'll take care of it."

I had no idea how he was going to pull this off.

"But the *Saganit* told us that she had no room in any of the four classes of grade nine," I said.

"Don't worry. She'll put another desk in one of the classes."

On the day before school was to begin, Reb Shraga called me into his office.

"Have your daughter come here to the *Yeshiva* at 8:30 tomorrow morning, dressed in a *Chadash* school uniform. I'm going to take her to school."

Miriam later told me what happened.

Reb Shraga took her to the *Chadash*, where he met the *Saganit*. His appearance there disturbed her greatly. She was visibly seething. Reb Shraga sat down in her office and told her that he had inspected a couple of the classrooms and noticed that there were empty desks.

"If Miriam isn't enrolled in a class very soon, I am going to seat her at a desk in one of the ninth-grade classrooms and I will sit next to her in that class every morning until she is," he said.

At the end of that first day the *Saganit* caved in. As did every other girl in the school, we finally had our "*protekzia*."

The fact that there were empty desks for Reb Shraga and Miriam to sit at, gave the lie to the *Saganit's* excuses. She explained to Rav Shraga that she was saving them for girls who were supposed to be coming soon from the United States— daughters of people who were very influential in the *charedie* world. Those supposed students never came.

While it was a traumatic beginning for my daughter, it worked out, in a sense, in the end. She did get an excellent education, but she also became very critical of some of the values taught and she wasn't afraid to respectfully express her views to her teachers.

On many occasions her teachers would emphasize the importance of women working to support their husbands and sons in their Torah learning. Although the Torah itself requires the husband to support his wife and family, the opposite was and still is a central message in the education of girls and young women in the *charedie* world. In Miriam's day the only profession open to young Israeli women in that world was teaching. Everyone who graduated was expected to become a teacher in the *Bais Yaacov* system and support their growing families on their income. The problem was that the salary for a teacher at the time was only about $1000 per month. To maintain a poverty level existence for a family of four a monthly income of about $1500, excluding rent or mortgage payments, was needed. Of course, families in the *charedie* community had an average of 8-10 children. Miriam knew these facts.

She recounted one such exchange with a teacher, after the teacher had again emphasized the importance of supporting their husbands and children by becoming teachers.

Miriam raised her hand and said:

"It's all well and good for you to tell us that we should become teachers to support our husbands and families. But you come from a wealthy family and your parents probably bought you an apartment and help you out with your monthly expenses. But not all of us have wealthy parents. We'll have to pay rent, electricity, gas, and water and buy food and all the other expenses of a household without help from family. And even if we could get a job as a teacher, we couldn't possibly support our families on that salary. And, as you know, there are thousands of *Bais Yaacov* graduates every year in Jerusalem alone. There are only enough teaching jobs for a tiny fraction of them. And, as I'm sure you also know, getting a job as a teacher in a *Bais Yaacov* is totally dependent on *"protekzia"*—knowing the right people. Why shouldn't we be realistic and get jobs as professionals in other fields so that we can make that dream of supporting our families a reality?"

I was very proud of the fact that Miriam had the courage to stand up and say what she thought needed to be said. She would have made an excellent lawyer.

Her teacher accused her of being of little faith. To work at any other job would jeopardize their status of *"bas melech"*—a princess. And to work in other professions with men in the same office was something that a princess should never do.

I sided with my daughter.

It is interesting to note that a few years after she graduated, the *Chadash* was turning out CPAs and bookkeepers at an astounding rate. Now, in addition, they train young women to be architects, computer programmers, etc.—jobs that can afford them the ability to support their husbands and families.

But that change in policy was too late for my daughter. She went to college and graduate school and became a social worker and therapist (serving the religious community) in defiance of what she was taught in school.

Another pet peeve of Miriam's was the school's concentration on the rules of *"tznius"*—modesty. The Torah says next to nothing about this subject. Its laws and customs are almost entirely rabbinic. They are inferred from the laws of the *"sotah"*—the suspected unfaithful wife.

If there is no evidence or insufficient evidence to convict her of being unfaithful in a court of law, her husband had the right to bring her to the Temple in Jerusalem for a trial by ordeal. She was forced to drink water in which parchment containing the text of the Torah regarding this sin had been dissolved. If she was guilty, certain physical manifestations of her sin appeared on her body and soon afterward she would die. The priest administering the ordeal loosened her garments and uncovered her hair and part of her body was exposed. From here many rules regarding *tznius* are derived.

While unmarried girls are allowed to show their hair, they are not allowed to expose their bodies. The question is what does exposure mean? If one studies the compilations of Jewish Law throughout the millennia, these rules change according to place and time. In Arab countries, Jewish women were required to completely cover their bodies and faces. In European countries the covering was less. Over time and with changing fashions, the rules also changed. According to the rules of the *Chadash*, not only was the length of sleeves and hem of the dress regulated, but also the denier of the stockings. These rules were quite detailed, and although most were not found in the Code of Jewish Law, a violation of them would risk expulsion. A squad of young "religious" men who enjoyed hanging out in town—at malls, movie theaters and cafes—were employed by the *"Mishmeres HaTznius"*—the "Modesty Patrol." They would spy on the *Bais Yaacov girls*, photograph them in "compromising circumstances" and then report them to the school. What were these "compromising circumstances"? Among them were talking to boys in the street (even if he was her brother); or if they had unbuttoned the top button of their blouse in the hot summer months; or if they had a pocketbook with a long strap. As absurd as some of these rules might seem, the school stressed them much more than the laws of *loshon hara*—speaking ill of others, or tattling, which the Torah forbids as a very grave sin. The behavior of girls who formed exclusive cliques or acted with meanness toward other girls who were not in their "in group"; or who spoke derogatorily about other girls, etc. was ignored. My daughter felt that the school, instead of teaching the Torah's emphasis on proper conduct in interpersonal relationships, concentrated on externalities that had very little to do with Jewish Law. I applauded her criticism and encouraged her to point out these inconsistencies to her teachers.

Rochel Malka seemed to fit in well with her classmates in her kindergarten. While Miriam had learned Hebrew in school in Cleveland, Rochi was only four years old when we moved and had no Hebrew skills. But after six months in the country, both were fluent. I would leave the *Yeshiva* at about 1 pm and hurry to the Bukharin neighborhood to be at her school when it ended at 1:15 p.m. I *davened mincha* in one of the local *shuls* with Rochi in tow. Then we would wend our way down a steep hill and then up another to Maalot Dafne. We would often stop on our way at a *pita* bakery on Yoel Street, which was next to the *shul*. It was one of the "must see" sites in Jerusalem. The bakery, which was probably at least a hundred years old, was owned by an old Iraqi husband and wife, who were its sole workers. The space it occupied was tiny, the size of a small room and completely open to the street. The whole baking process was done by hand and the oven was the same type as was used in *Gemara* times, two thousand years ago. Jewish law is replete with descriptions of the baking process as it was in the old days. *Pitot*, the round loaves of bread that are so popular now all over the world, were not baked on trays in what we know as an oven, but in an oven that was cone shaped—wide at the bottom and narrow at the top, to retain the heat. Dough was slapped onto the sides of the oven, almost vertically and then peeled off when baked. The only difference between the oven we saw in Bukharin and the ones described in the *Gemara* was the heat source. Originally it had been wood, but now it was gas. A very, very hot fire was constantly burning at the bottom of the oven and the baker, after mixing the flour and water and shaping it into a flat pancake and leaving it to rise for a half hour or so, would take a leather pillow and slap the pancake onto the wall of the oven. After a minute he'd peel off the pita and sell it. Crowds of customers would stand outside in the narrow street and patiently wait for their turn to buy. The *pitot* was renowned throughout the city.

After returning home from school, the first thing that Miriam and Rochi would do, was to go to the end of the parking lot of our building where a family of Arabs lived and where they kept their colorfully decorated camels. They were in the business of giving camel rides to tourists in the Old City, which was only a thirty-minute walk from our house, or a fifteen-minute camel ride. The girls loved to watch the camels.

In those days, there was no paved road separating Arab East Jerusalem from the Western part, only a huge field that stretched for miles to the Old City's Damascus Gate. Every morning Arab shepherds would graze their sheep in the field right past our living room window. It was otherworldly and magical. We were living in both the modern world and the ancient one, with no discernable separation. It was something like my view of the Temple Mount from Hebrew University. A window to the ancient world from the modern one.

After that first year in kindergarten, Rochi joined Miriam in the *Bais Yaacov of Sanhedria Murchevet* for elementary school. Rochi enjoyed her elementary and high schools without much drama.

CHAPTER XIV
Binyamin's Schooling

When Binyamin turned four it was time to find a *cheder* (a boy's religious elementary school) for him. Having had the experience with Miriam, I went straight to my *Rosh Yeshiva* and *rebbe*, Rav Amram Blackman and asked him for his advice and help in placing my son. He suggested *Hadar Zion*, a nearby *cheder*, about a seven-minute walk from our apartment. I had heard about another *cheder*, Zilberman's, in the Old City, which sounded good to me. The boys there memorize the *Chumash* and *Navi* (the Bible and Prophets) and they learn *mishnayos* before they start learning *Gemara*. I thought this was the ideal way to educate a boy. But others talked me out of it. Yes, they said, it's a good system, but if a boy is unhappy there, he won't fit into another *cheder* since he'd be years behind in learning *Gemara*. Also, that school met every day, even on *Shabbos and Yom tov*. If you didn't live in the Old City, it was impractical for your son to get to school on those days and then he'd be behind. Also, it's a very punishing schedule. There were basically no days off. We sent him to *Hadar Tzion*.

By the third grade, Binyamin was very unhappy at school. He was a very sweet boy and with two older sisters and one younger sister, was neither aggressive nor violent. He complained about the wildness of the other boys in the class and was afraid to leave his classroom at recess. I met with his *rebbe* and the *menahal* (principal) of the *cheder*. They both reassured me that everything was fine. Binyamin would feel more comfortable as time went on. They suggested hiring a tutor for him, a Rav Geter, who was a teaching assistant there. Rav Geter was a wonderful help. Binyamin loved him and developed a warm and personal relationship that lasted throughout his teen years. As to his fear of the other kids in the class, I understood it immediately as I waited to meet with the *menahel*. It was wintertime and at recess all the boys ran into the large entrance hall of the school and fighting erupted. It wasn't just pushing or shoving, but a serious melee. Boys were kicking and punching each other as if they were rival gangs except there were no discernable battle lines—just one giant ball of kids with arms and legs flailing, hitting whoever they could. The *rebbes* were standing off to the side smoking cigarettes and chatting with their colleagues as if what was going on was the most normal thing in the world. When I brought it up to the *menahel*, he assured me that no kids are seriously hurt and fighting builds character and prepares them for life in Israel. Not being an Israeli, I couldn't argue his last point, but thought it did explain a lot about Israel that I didn't like.

I sent Binyamin to karate classes. I didn't want him to feel afraid of the other kids. His *dojo* was run by a former IDF *krav megav* (an Israeli version of karate) instructor. Binyamin went for a few years. He became good at it, advanced rapidly and won several competitions. He lost his fear of the other boys, but then had a new problem. Once the boys in his school found out that he was learning *krav megav*, they all wanted to fight him. The problem was that his karate master forbade his students to use what he taught them against others who hadn't learned it. He was afraid that they might kill someone. Binyamin took his admonition to heart and refused to fight. After a couple of months of being beaten up every day we moved him to another *cheder—Sanhedrin,* which was about a fifteen-minute walk from home. He made sure not to tell anyone about his karate classes and the boys were a lot less aggressive and violent than in *Hadar Zion.* He was much happier there.

For *Yeshiva Katana* (junior high and high school) we chose one in *Maale Michmash,* a *moshav* (settlement) in the Shomron (aka the "West Bank"). The *Rosh HaYeshiva* was a well-known American educator who believed in giving the boys an excellent religious and secular education. Unfortunately, it closed after two years and we were forced to find another place for Binyamin Tzvi, which was probably a good thing. During his second year, 2002, the Palestinians had begun the Second Intifada. *Maale Michmash* is situated near Ramalah, the seat of the Palestinian government. Every night the boys in the *yeshiva* were treated to a sound and light show by the IDF raining bombs and bullets on the Arab terrorists. While this might have had a debilitating effect on the Arabs, it also instilled great fear in many of the boys. My son had difficulty sleeping and he often came home because he wasn't feeling well, a diagnosis of PTSD would probably be warranted. War is not healthy for anyone even if one is not in immediate danger. For teenagers its effects can have lasting consequences. He did, however, form many solid friendships there, which he maintains to this day, over 20 years later.

The next year Binyamin attended a *Yeshiva Katana* in the Geula neighborhood of Jerusalem. But with all the distractions of the center of the city and his previous experience in school, his education was floundering. Before he turned seventeen, he quit school and together with his best friend and next-door neighbor, went to work as a plumber's assistant.

By the time Binyamin had turned 18 and was drafted into the Army, his religious observance had slackened. He was still the wonderful son he always had been, but I was very worried about his future as a *frum* Jew.

The Army turned him around. He was motivated to excel and applied for admission to the Paratroopers—one of the elite combat units in the IDF. It was also a magnet for boys from *Hesder Yeshivot* (Zionistic post high schools), which emphasize combat service in the Armed Forces. He was selected and was assigned to the Unit known as 101. His unit was about forty percent religious, and their base camp had a majority of religious soldiers. Because of peer pressure, *minyanim* were almost compulsory. Instead of lying in bed and sleeping through *shacharis,* as he did at home, Binyamin became a *shul* goer. His prior lack of motivation had been replaced by a drive for excellence in all aspects of his Army life. He was an exemplary soldier and was promoted to the highest ranks of enlisted men. Just as my father, *a'h* was a high-ranking sergeant in the American Army, so was his namesake, Binyamin Tzvi, in the IDF. He loved the Army while he was there, although not enough to make it a career.

The Army in Israel is quite different than in many other countries. In some ways it's like the Scouts and college and your extended family all rolled into one. Soldiers are made to feel that they are part of a club. Retired members of the 101 regularly returned to the base bearing presents and hosting barbecues. Through various support organizations, American Jews sent stenciled backpacks, expensive military watches and other dazzling swag. They also regularly had pizzas delivered to those on guard duty.

Army service in Israel is compulsory for three years. At the end of the training period, which for a combat soldier can take up to a year, soldiers are urged to return home almost every weekend. At most bus stops on Sunday morning, you see crowds of soldiers on their way to the Central Bus Station to return to their bases.

Parents and families are encouraged to be present at all the major events in their child's service. We were invited to Binyamin's swearing-in ceremony at the Western Wall in Jerusalem; the celebration of the end of basic training at his army base—where he received his paratrooper wings and his red beret; and the completion of his ninety-mile nonstop hike from one end of the country to the other, which ended up in our neighborhood in Jerusalem. We live in Maalot Dafna, the site of one of the major battles of the Six Day War in 1967—Ammunition Hill. On that hill, the Jordanian Army, which controlled the area from 1948, had dug extensive trenchworks bristling with heavy machine guns. It commanded a wide area below. My son's Paratroop unit—the 101, sustained very heavy casualties in taking that hill. Soon after Israel's victory in 1967 that part of the hill, with the trenchworks, became a national monument and a memorial to the Paratroopers of Unit 101 who died there. On many *Shabbatot,* when Binyamin and his sisters were young, we would go there for walks. The kids would play hide and seek in the trenches and climb all over the tank on display. It's no wonder our son ended up in that unit.

The Army also provided him with courses in secular studies that were not available in his *yeshivos*, to prepare him for his *Bagrut*—his High School diploma.

Finally, the Army provided the stage for his proposal to his future wife. At the end of the ceremony on Ammunition Hill, celebrating the 90-mile hike, the *emcee,* a major in the unit, made an announcement to the hundreds of people there.

"Don't leave yet," he said to the crowd over the loudspeakers. "We have one more announcement to make. Miri Flatow, please come to the podium."

Miri was my son's first and only girlfriend. He had known her since he was sixteen and she was fourteen. She was a shy high school girl of seventeen on that day and froze in her tracks when she heard her name called. The crowd began to chant. "Miri, Miri, Miri."

After shaking herself out of her stupor, she made her way to the center stage. My son was there with balloons and a big sign that said: "MIRI WILL YOU MARRY ME?". He handed the sign to one of his comrades and got down on one knee, took out a ring and held it in front of her. She would have said "yes" even without the crowd, but now what choice did she have? She said "yes" and the crowd went wild. Say what you will about my son, but he doesn't take after me. I have serious stage fright.

After the Army and his marriage to Miri, Binyamin expressed a sincere desire to return to *yeshiva* and make up for all those lost years. With his small pension from the army and my help, he was able to learn, uninterruptedly, without needing to work, for three years in Ohr HaTzadikim. He loved his time there and was an outstanding student. And I should know. I kept close tabs on him since I knew all his *rabbeim*. In his last year he joined our graduate program, which prepares young men for *smicha,* the rabbinate, *kiruv* and teaching careers. My son is a natural teacher and loves teaching kids. He would have made a wonderful teacher, but to support his growing family he needed a more lucrative line of work. He found it in glass design and installation. His teaching skills aren't wasted. He leads youth groups and helps his kids with their homework.

CHAPTER XV
Yocheved's Education

By the time our youngest was ready for school, we were old hands in the educational system, or so we thought. We sent Yochi to a Sephardic *Bait Yaacov* for elementary and junior high school. In a way, I suppose, we were honoring my wife's Sephardic heritage. Since our older girls weren't thrilled with the Ashkenazi *Beis Yaacov* schools they attended, it sounded like a plan.

    The school was laid back. The girls had fun. There wasn't a great emphasis on academics. The dress code was more relaxed. Unfortunately, Yochi didn't learn much there. She chose to go to the more academic Rappaport high school, which was an American-style Ashkenazi *Beis Yaacov*. Almost all the girls were English speakers, and many were born or lived overseas. It was less strict than the Israeli *Bais Yaacovs* and Mrs. Rappaport was friendly and understanding. Yochi made many lasting friendships there.

    After finishing high school, she spent a year studying fashion design and sewing, thinking that she might become a fashion designer. After that year she joined *Sherut Leumi*—a national program which is an alternative to Army service. She spent a year tutoring English-speaking immigrant children who needed extra help with their Hebrew language skills and schoolwork. She worked at various jobs for a couple of years after that and then went back to school to complete her *Bagrut* in order to matriculate into university. She spent the next three years at Ariel University where she earned degrees in Criminology and Psychology.

My dream for her was to be a detective in the police department. I could picture myself helping her solve unsolvable crimes. I had vast knowledge of the field myself since I had read all of Sherlock Holmes and watched many detective movies and TV shows over the years.

But, alas, that was not to be. The police didn't accept her application to join the force as a detective and she worked for another two years directing an NGO for battered Israeli and Arab women and was a founder of an NGO for battered women from Somalia.

In 2020, she moved to London for a master's degree in Health Psychology at University College London, consistently rated as one of the top universities in the world. She graduated in 2021.

CHAPTER XVI
Miriam and Rochi
Back to Cleveland

After Miriam and Rochi graduated from high school, I sent them to Yavne Seminary in Cleveland. When we lived in Cleveland, I had been the President of the Seminary, which meant that I gave them generous donations. But I had also developed a close relationship with the Headmistress, Rebbitzen Chaya Ausband. Rabbi and Rebbitzen Ausband lived on Yeshiva Lane in Wickliffe and in my frequent attendance at the Telshe Yeshiva, I had gotten to know them. Both were from Lithuania and had lived in the village of Telshe. They both miraculously survived the Nazi invasion of Lithuania. Rabbi Ausband was a genius and great scholar who I had heard was a *Dayan* (Judge of the Rabbinic Court) in Telshe at the age of 19. His *rebbetzin* was the daughter of the Telshe *Rosh HaYeshiva*, Reb Yosef Bloch. She was also brilliant. She told me that she had gone to Jewish high school in Lithuania, where they learned all their Hebrew studies in *Ivris*—classical Hebrew with an Ashkenazic pronunciation. Their secular education was not ignored, and they studied history, literature, sciences and mathematics and even calculus. She was, of course, fluent in Hebrew. Her school in Cleveland, Yavne, bore the same name as her *alma mater* in Lithuania. To say that Yavne Seminary in Cleveland was a post high school teacher's training school would be a vast understatement. Yavne was the Harvard of seminaries and probably quite a bit harder than Harvard. There is no women's seminary in the world that had a teacher like "*Morah*" (the Teacher) as she was called by her students. Her specialty was *Ramban* (Nachmanides). She guided the girls through the *Chumash* with the *Ramban* and stressed his grammatical commentaries—comments that I would skip over because of their difficulty.

She also taught the girls *Shiurei Daas*—a multi-volume philosophical text authored by her father, which, because I had studied in Telshe Yeshiva, I had become aware of and had been introduced to some of its contents by my *chavrusa*, Rabbi Aryeh Levine. But, when it came to reading it myself, it was a mystery. The language was obscure, and concepts were very esoteric. When, on occasion, I tried to decipher it, I had to ask Miriam to help me.

Both Miriam and Rochi had a very rigorous year in Yavne and gained tremendously from the experience. They also met and made lasting friendships with their classmates.

CHAPTER XVII
Dr. Nechemia Schein

Since I mentioned Lithuania, and since my family background is also from that small area in the Pale of Settlement, I think it's appropriate to mention another survivor of the Kovno ghetto, one that had a major influence on our family, Dr. Nechemia Shein, also known to my children as Uncle Nechemia, who was a frequent guest at our home in Cleveland and Jerusalem.

His family, like most Jewish families in Kovno in the 1920s and '30s was religious. They were not as rigorous in their observance as the families of the nearby Telshe Yeshiva, but still quite observant. In the early 1930s Lithuania in general and Kovno in particular, was a center of the *haskalah* (enlightenment) movement, with a decidedly Zionistic bent. Nechemia went to a school where the instruction, in most subjects, even the secular ones, was in Modern Hebrew. So, in addition to Yiddish, Hebrew became almost a mother tongue. Literature and philosophy were taught in the language of the particular author they were studying. Goethe, Heine, Schiller, etc. were all taught in German. French and Russian literature was taught in their respective languages. By the time his education was interrupted by the German invasion and the destruction of the Lithuanian Jewish community, at the age of thirteen, Nechemia was already fluent in French, German, Russian, Yiddish, Hebrew, and Lithuanian. In mathematics and the sciences, the instruction was years ahead of the level common in the rest of Europe. In fact, after the war, when he took the entrance exams to medical school in Germany, without having been in school since he was thirteen, and certainly with no access or time to read books in Auschwitz and Dachau, he was able to pass them without any difficulty. And Nechemia wasn't the only one. Other boys of his age from Lithuania who managed to survive the camps also were admitted to medical schools in Germany after a rigorous entrance exam with only their 9th and 10th grade educations.

Nechemia came from a prosperous family. His father was a businessman and arms dealer, who sold munitions to the Lithuanian Army. Before the Second World War, the country was run by an oligarchy that solicited bribes from those doing business with the government and embezzled money from the Central Bank. One way of doing this was buying fictitious *materiel* for the army, paying the bill of lading, and then splitting the money with the supplier, Nechemia's father. This system worked fine until there was a new minister of defense who wasn't part of the scheme and suspecting illegal behavior, decided to spring a surprise audit of the country's main armory. Because he had befriended well-placed officials in key positions, Nechemia's father heard about the surprise audit the night before it was to happen. Nechemia remembers his father leaving home in the middle of the night and then being awakened as the night was split by a series of explosions that sounded as if the world was blowing up. His father came home soon afterwards and told him not to worry, but that he had met with the top generals of the country, and they had decided to blow up the armory in a "accident" that destroyed any hope of a proper audit.

Nechemia was a studious boy and learned his lessons well

both in *limudei kodesh* and *chol* (religious and secular subjects). His mother, a religious woman, liked his devotion to Torah and *mitzvohs* but cautioned him. "I want you to be religious like a Rov not like a shoemaker." She explained. "The Rov, if it's pouring rain outside, *davens* at home and stays dry, the shoemaker goes to *shul* and gets soaked to his skin. "

In 1940, the Nazis rounded up all the Jews in Kovno and moved them to a place called the "Ninth Fort." They were ordered to dig a large pit, which was to be their grave, lined them up and machine-gunned them all. Nechemia and his father were among them. But they fell into the pit a moment before being shot. They played dead. The rest of their family was murdered there. After dark, Nechemia and his father escaped the pit of the dead and dying and ran to the countryside. Their salvation lasted only for a few days until some Lithuanians found them and turned them over to the Nazis. They were deported to Auschwitz, tattooed, and sent to a work camp. Nechamia, now a fourteen-year-old, a time of youthful rebellion and idealism had two objectives; to keep his father (who was not very healthy) alive and safe and to maintain his own identity in a Nazi world that was designed to strip the Jew of his.

I asked Nechemia many times how he got the long and prominent scar encircling his neck. He always changed the subject. But after months of pestering, he finally told me. One afternoon the camp commandant, an SS Colonel with shiny black leather riding boots and a meticulous Nazi uniform, told him to kiss his boots. Fourteen-year-old Nechemia refused. He was not going to disgrace himself in front of his enemy. The Nazi took out his Luger and pointed it at Nechemia's head and told him to kiss his boots. Nechemia refused and spit on the boots instead. Jews, of course, were killed for no reason at all and here there was ample reason to pull the trigger at such flagrant insubordination. However, the Nazi holstered his gun and ordered that Nechemia be hung to make "an example" of him to the rest of the camp. The method of hanging was from a pole and with piano wire. Nechemia was hoisted up by his neck as the wire cut deeply into it. After half a minute, the Commandant ordered that he be let down. His neck was bleeding from the gash made by the wire, but otherwise he was uninjured. While he would never know the reason, Nechemia's explanation was that the Nazi commandant had seen the courage of the Jewish teenager and respected it. Another and more logical explanation would be that G-d had decided to keep him alive.

One day the Nazis brought into Nechemia's barracks a newly arrived contingent of Dutch Jews. They seemed particularly jolly, and dangerously so. The camps were no places to relax if you wished to stay alive. The Dutchmen were ordered out of the barracks to go to work, but the Nazis had taken their shoes upon their arrival, and they were barefoot. A vote was taken, and they all decided to "strike" until they got their shoes back. Nechemia was horrified and told them that the Nazis would shoot them on the spot if they didn't go out to work. They just laughed and sat on their bunks and told him, "No shoes, no work." Nechemia pleaded with them not to be foolish and get themselves killed. The Dutchmen just laughed until the Nazi guards came in and shot them all dead in their bunks.

Toward the end of the war in Europe the Allies had been successfully bombing the German arms factories. So, the Germans started building their factories underground to protect them from the air war. Nechemia and his father were now in

Dachau, near Munich where they were building a ball bearing factory underground. To do so, the Jews steered heavy wheelbarrows filled with wet cement from ground level to the floor far below, by means of winding earthen ramps. One day when Nechemia was near the top of the ramp and his father was near the bottom, his father's strength gave out and his wheelbarrow tilted over, and the cement spilled out. The Nazi guard beat his father with his rifle. Seeing this from above, Nechemia made a quick decision and aimed his wheelbarrow at the guard and pushed it over the edge of the ramp. It landed next to the Nazi without harming him. The guard ordered Nechemia down to the ground level and took out his pistol to shoot. Enraged and bewildered, he asked Nechemia why he did what he did. Nechemia looked at him in the eye and said, "That was my father you were beating. If you saw someone beating your father like that, what would you do?" Incredibly and miraculously, the Nazi considered the question and answered him: "I would have done the same." From then on, until the liberation, that Nazi guard gave him and his father extra rations and treated them with unusual kindness and respect.

After the war, Nechemia and his father were in a Displaced Persons' camp in Southern Germany. Nechemia was admitted to the Medical School in Marburg, Germany. As I mentioned, he had learned enough German Literature, Math, and Science in primary school to pass the entrance exams. One afternoon he went to a movie theater. Before the movie there was a newsreel. In Germany, under the occupation of the Allies, it was a policy to show the Germans the horrors they inflicted on the Jews. All newsreels included clips of the concentration and death camps. A German sitting a few rows in front of him started cheering when the corpses of dead Jews about to be incinerated were shown. He shouted out, "Hitler should have killed them all." After the movie Nechemia followed the man out of the theater and into an alley and attacked him. As he was beating the German, a patrol of American soldiers happened by and arrested Nechemia and took the German to the hospital. Nechemia explained why he beat the German to the investigating officer who let him go with a warning.

Nechemia was the Vice President of the Jewish Students Union of Europe. Although he was officially stateless, that position afforded him papers issued by the Allies allowing him to travel all over Europe. It also acted as a cover for a more important job, procuring arms for the fledgling army of the future state of Israel in their fight against all the Arab nations arrayed against it. He managed to buy huge amounts of weapons and *materiel* mostly from Czechoslovakia and smuggle them out of Europe through Marseille. As an agent for the Irgun, he met many times with Menachem Begin. In one planning session he suggested that Israel, after independence, should ally itself with Stalin, who would then let it do what it wanted with the Arabs, whereas the Americans, especially the State Department, were very anti-Semitic and inclined to side with our enemies. Begin, a rabid anti-communist, rejected not just the idea, but also Nechemia. As a result, after the war, instead of settling in Israel, Nechemia and his father moved to Cleveland, Ohio, where I met him. He worked as a doctor in the famed Cleveland Clinic. A few years after we made *Aliyah,* Nechemia also did. He would visit us often until his death in 2010.

CHAPTER XVIII
A New Profession

In the late 1990's I entered a new profession—*Shadchanus* (matchmaking). It happened by chance. A friend of mine, Rabbi Boruch Schmidt, whom I had known as a student at Ohr HaTzadikim, was teaching at our sister school, Nof Yerushalayim, a women's seminary in the Har Nof neighborhood of Jerusalem. He was also their unofficial *shadchan*. As a *rebbe* at the *Yeshiva*, I was quite close to many of the students. A main preoccupation of the older ones was finding a wife—a *shidduch*. We regularly hosted girls from various seminaries at our *Shabbos* table when we didn't have *yeshiva* boys eating with us. I had managed to make a few *shidduchim* between our guys and Nof girls. It wasn't a profession yet, just a hobby. Reb Boruch called me one day to announce that because of time constraints, he had decided to give up his active *shadchanus* business and asked if I was interested in taking it over. I thought about it for a few seconds and answered in the affirmative.

"Good," he said. "From now on I'm going to send you all my Nof girls."

But first—an introduction to the world of *shidduchim* in the World of Religious Jews.

CHAPTER XIX
Marriage Customs Among Orthodox Jews

The Ashkenazic Orthodox Jewish World in America, Israel, England, and most countries where larger populations of religious Jews are found, is made up of three main groups: Modern Orthodox; *Yeshivish* (also known as *Litvish*) and *Chassidish*. There are also the Sephardim (Jews from the Spanish Diaspora), Eastern Communities (Syria, Iraq, and Persia) and the *Temanim* (Yemen and Aden). Each of them has subdivisions, but I'm going to focus on the larger groupings of the Ashkenazim in America and Israel.

The Modern Orthodox, which in Israel is called *Dati Leumi* (National Religious), is probably the largest group. It consists essentially of those Jews who are very traditional, keep *Shabbat and kashrut* and have learnt in religious schools, but whose lives are largely integrated into the secular world. In Israel this means obtaining a *Bagrut* (a high-level high school diploma), going into the army at 18 and afterwards attending university or working, depending on one's academic inclination.

University graduates go into the various professions—law, medicine, engineering, finance, computers, teaching, business, etc. In America it is essentially the same without army service. Again, there is an emphasis on a secular education. In both America and Israel, *shidduchim* in this group are not that different from that in secular society, except for meeting potential mates by chance in bars. Many meet their future spouses at single events at *shul* or through friends and family members. Parental involvement is usually minimal. Our two older daughters, who were essentially in this group, and worked for a religious Jewish social welfare agency, met their future spouses through work related events in the States.

In the Yeshivish World of Israel, schooling is almost entirely religious. For boys up to the age of thirteen, the school day begins at around 7:30 a.m. and continues to 5:00 to 6:00 p.m. They learn rudimentary science, arithmetic, and geography, but the main emphasis is on *Chumash, Mishnayos, Halacha and Gemara*. After bar mitzvah, at thirteen, most of them go to boarding school (called *Yeshiva Katana*), where the *Gemara* learning is from early in the morning until late at night. Some time is also allotted to learning *Halacha* and *mussar* (ethics). Secular studies are mostly absent.

The girls, as I described above in telling my daughter Miriam's story, have a much broader secular education, but the focus is on religious studies. They generally live at home and their school day ends at about 1:30 p.m.

In America, boys from *yeshivishe* homes go to day school or *yeshiva* (as it is called in New York) for primary school and then to *yeshiva* high school. While the main emphasis is on religious studies, they also complete the necessary secular classwork that is required in the state where they reside and graduate with a state sanctioned high school diploma.

After high school boys continue in *Yeshiva* where the learning is often very intense—three *sedarim* a day—from early in the morning to 10:30 p.m. or so at night. Some boys go off to Israel to study in *Yeshivos* for several years and then come back to the States. When they do return, they will often go to *Beis Medrash Govoha* in Lakewood, New Jersey, which with about 5000 students, is the largest *yeshiva* in America. After a six-month stay in the "freezer" (the term used for their inactive dating status) they thaw out and are permitted to start dating. Matches are made almost exclusively through *shadchanim*. *Yeshivishe* young men are a very dear commodity, because not all who start off primary school will finish as solid *yeshiva bochurim*. Many boys are turned off by the strictness of the regime and the long hours of studying and don't make it into the "freezer". Also, many teenage boys have difficulty controlling their raging hormones and they find a monkish life difficult. There are smaller numbers who fall by the wayside, but stay religious, and others who leave observance altogether.

Yeshivishe girls, also known as *Bais Yaacov* girls, are more plentiful. Girls, in general, tend to be less rebellious and the emphasis of their schools is to mold them into modest, attractive young *maidelach* (maidens). They are more social beings than young men and rather less competitive. The concentration on religious studies, although strong, is much less than with boys. And, in general, *Bais Yaacov* girls in the States go to college. The object is to get a profession that they can work at full time before they have children and then work part time after having children—thus, being able to support a husband while he's learning in *yeshiva*. In the U.S. the preferred professions for women are physical therapist, speech therapist, and occupational therapist.

One needn't be nerdish to be a *Bais Yaacov* girl, while it helps to be so for a Yeshivish boy. As a result of this imbalance, it is said that eligible *Bais Yaacov* girls need a PR agent while eligible *yeshiva* boys need a secretary.

In Israel the situation is similar, except that women tend to go into fields where contact with men is limited—like accounting, bookkeeping, architecture, computer programming and teaching. The objective is the same—to be able to support her husband while he's learning and have time to take care of the children. Traditionally, *Charedie* women did not go to university, but in recent years *charedie* colleges, which are segregated by sex, have opened and it is becoming more acceptable for women to get a higher education.

In the *Chassidishe* World boys generally have no secular education beyond simple arithmetic. The language of instruction in both America and Israel is *Yiddish*, and fluency of speech or ability to read or write in English in the U.S. is severely limited. In Israel they speak, read, and write Hebrew fluently, since Hebrew is the language of the streets and almost all religious texts. They stay in *yeshiva* until they get married and then, depending on their sect of *Chassidus,* will learn for a year or two and then go to work.

Girls in the *Chassidishe* world both in the States and in Israel have very limited secular education, and as most *Chassidish* men work, they don't need a profession to support their husbands. If they are business minded, they might go into a retail business or help their husband in his business.

Shidduchim for *Chassidim* may come from suggestions of family members or s*hadchanim* or from their *rebbe* and his family. Marrying cousins is quite common. Money is not usually a main issue in finding a spouse. Generally, both sides are poor and will struggle to meet their obligations. In Israel parents are less likely to promise an apartment to the couple but will pledge money for rent.

First Dates
The Yeshiva World

In Israel, in the *Yeshiva* World, before the prospective couple meet, the parents sit down together to "talk *tachlis*"—money. It is customary for a young couple to receive an apartment, furniture and appliances and a monthly stipend from the parents. The parents of an outstanding *bochur (single young man)* in Israel might hold out for a *siddur maaleh*—the full package from the girl's family—the wedding, a furnished apartment in Jerusalem with a generous monthly stipend. But more commonly, the costs will be split down the middle—both sides contributing an equal amount. This means that both sides are in the same economic bracket, since there is no way that a poor man can even borrow enough to match the rich man's 50%. Once the money is out of the way, the two young people can meet. They customarily go out as many as five or six times before they decide one way or the other.

In America, in the *Yeshiva* World the parents don't usually meet each other before the first date. The *shadchan* will be familiar with the economic situation of both parties and will find out what each is prepared to do to finance the new couple's life, but details will be sorted out later, if their two children like each other and want to proceed.

The Chassidishe World

The first date in the *Chassidishe* World is also the last date. The following is typical for a *Chassidishe shidduch*. A friend of mine, Mendel, an American *Belzer Chassid* living in Israel for the last 40 years, told me the following story about his son's match.

It was *Shavuos* morning in the large, beautiful, and new *Belzer Beis Medrash* in Jerusalem. After *davening*, the custom is for the thousands of *Chassidim* present to file past the *Rebbe* and wish him a *"gut yontif"*—a happy holiday. Mendel approached the *Rebbe*, shook his hand, and wished him *a gut yontif.* The *Rebbe* held onto Mendel's hand and told him to wait until the line ended. He wanted to speak to him. A half hour later the *Rebbe* introduced him to another *Chassid*—Mr. Goldberg who was recently divorced and was visiting from New York with his single daughter. The *Rebbe* suggested that Mendel's son might be interested in the *shidduch,* and they should meet tomorrow evening at Mr. Goldberg's sister's apartment.

A suggestion from the *Rebbe* is like a command, and if the *Rebbe* is suggesting a *shidduch*, it's as if *Hashem* himself is telling the *Chassid* that this match is perfect. Shiya was nineteen and this was his first date and Mendel's first experience with *shidduchim.*

"We got to the apartment at around 10:00 pm and the first thing I noticed was that the women in the kitchen were cutting up cake and fruit to serve at the *l'chaim*—the pre-engagement party. My son and Goldberg's daughter went into the living room alone while we were all in the kitchen with the food. After about twenty minutes my son came into the kitchen and gave his mother and me a thumbs up. He was now engaged. We called the *Rebbe* who came over for the *l'chaim.*"

The custom among *Chassidim* is to wait for a year between the engagement and wedding without any in-person contact between the couple. The only communication they have is by phone, mail, or fax. A year later Shiya and Fruma married. They are living happily ever after with a burgeoning family in Borough Park, Brooklyn.

It didn't work out so well for Yehudit who came to see me for a *shidduch*. Yehudit was twenty-five, beautiful, very smart—she was the COO of a high-tech company in Israel—and divorced. She had once been a *Chassida,* a member of a Chassidic sect.

She had grown up in a *Chassidishe* home in Antwerp. Her parents were *baalei teshuva.* The *Rebbe's* cousin, who lived in New York, called Yehudit's mother when Yehudit turned eighteen. She told her that she had heard all about Yehudit and how she was beautiful and intelligent and suggested a *shidduch* for her with a learned boy from a very wealthy and prominent family in Brooklyn. Yehudit's parents were honored by the involvement of a close relation of the *Rebbe* in their daughter's marriage plans. Yehudit also felt honored and was eager to meet her future *choson*—her bridegroom.

A few weeks later Moshe and his mother flew into Antwerp to meet his future *kallah* (bride) and her family. The scene was like the one Mendel described. The mothers were in the kitchen cutting up the cake and fruit while the young couple met in the parlor.

Yehudit recounted the conversation.

"Moshe was unusually quiet. I thought that he was inexperienced in dating, nervous and very modest. I asked him questions like how his trip was and how he liked Antwerp. He answered with very short phrases like "fine" or "very nice." I assumed that since in our world, where boys never talk to girls outside their immediate family, he found it difficult to talk to me. I also knew that the *Gemara* says that a man shouldn't speak too much to a woman, and certainly one who is not his wife. I assumed he was following that dictum. He looked presentable enough and after twenty minutes of stilted conversation, we came out, smiled, and shook our heads in agreement to the *shidduch*. The match was made, and mother and son left the next day.

During the year before the wedding, we communicated very often by mail and fax. His letters were poetic and intelligent with many quotes from *Tanach* and commentaries. I was very proud of my erudite and articulate *choson*. I anxiously anticipated the beautiful wedding that my parents planned. That happy day finally came. I had not seen my *choson* for a whole year and now we stood under the *chuppah* (the wedding canopy), ready to consecrate our match.

After the wedding ceremony we retired to the *yichud* (private) room where we had a small snack before the wedding festivities began. I had noticed that under the *chuppah* my *choson* seemed to be a bit "out of it". I attributed that to his nervousness. Once in the *yichud* room I asked him:

"How are you feeling? You look a little pale."

"How am I feeling?" he repeated.

"Are you all right?" I asked, with growing concern.

"Am I all right?" he answered with a silly smile on his face.

He seemed to be in a trance. I asked him some more questions and got similar responses. I surmised that he was heavily sedated."

The marriage ended right then and there. Yehudit was devastated. She left the *yichud* room in tears. Her mother took her home and she never saw Moshe again. Later she found out that he suffered from borderline retardation. He was also functionally illiterate. His mother had written all the lovely letters she received that year. Yehudit was the victim of an unfortunate scheme. Being seen as deficient, since her parents were *baalei teshuva*, she was given to someone in marriage who was also deficient—the thinking being that she should be happy to be a member of a prominent *chassidishe* family and at least her children or grandchildren would be accepted into the mainstream of *Chassidishe* society. The *Rebbe*, when informed about what his cousin had done, was outraged. He apologized profusely to Yehudit and her family and immediately arranged for her to receive a *get*—a divorce.

I told her I was amazed that she was still religious.

I'm sure that many young women or men in that same situation would have blamed Judaism for their fate. But, Yehudit's faith in G-d was strengthened through this experience. She was sadder but wiser and no longer a *Chassida*.

Yehudit's experience is not confined to the *Chassidishe* World. There are unscrupulous people everywhere. The fact that one dresses the part of the religious Jew doesn't mean that you can trust him implicitly. There are, unfortunately, charlatans and con men in every society, disguising themselves as righteous people—wolves in sheep's clothing. This is a lesson that can cost the *baal teshuva* or convert dearly, as Ruth found out.

Ruth came to see me after her divorce. She was a *geores* (female convert) from Minnesota. Although now in her early 50's she was still very attractive—tall and blonde, like her Norwegian ancestors. She had become interested in Judaism after her first husband died and with no children and a sizable nest egg, had decided, after her conversion in Minneapolis, to move to Jerusalem. She met Rabbi Tanover, a native

Yerushalmi, through a religious *shadchan*. She couldn't get over her good fortune. He was also a widower and seemed very interested in her. Although he spoke only broken English, his passion for her transcended speech. After a few dates she agreed to his proposal of marriage. Before the marriage he insisted that they buy an apartment in Meah Shearim, one of the most *charedie* neighborhoods in Jerusalem. The problem was, he claimed, that he had no ready money, but had recently received a registered letter from a lawyer in New York who was probating his rich uncle's estate. A very large inheritance would be his in another month or two. He would give Ruth his half when he got his money. She bought the apartment and had it registered in both names. Soon afterwards they had a small wedding in Meah Shearim.

Ruth was looking forward to the wedding night when she would finally be alone with her husband. They went to their new apartment together and she prepared for bed. Her new husband seemed to be in no hurry and was in the dining room drinking tea. Finally, he said to her: "Don't expect me to come to bed with you. Do you think that I, a rabbi, from a distinguished family would have anything to do with you—a *geores*? Sign over to me the other half of this apartment and I'll give you a *get*."

Heartbroken and chastened, she did. She found out later that she wasn't the only one he had hoodwinked. He had done it at least three times before and was now the owner of at least four apartments in Meah Shearim and quite a rich man. She now came to me looking for a proper *shidduch* with someone who was more realistic for her. Unfortunately, I had no one.

Of course, these are the horror stories. Most *shadchanim* would never take advantage of one of their clients or deceive them into making a match with a crook or someone totally unsuited. But this should serve as a warning to those who are too trusting. As the old Hebrew adage goes: "Honor him but be suspicious of him." Treat a person with respect but he must earn your trust.

In fact, it sometimes happens that the *shadchan* himself is taken in by a deceiver. It happened to me.

I set up Yosef, a *yeshiva* student and frequent guest at my home, with a number of eligible young women. I even tutored him for a half hour every day for almost a year. I prided myself on being a good judge of character and of detecting falsehoods in others. Yosef, in my eyes, was a prime catch. He was religious, outgoing, personable, intelligent, educated, athletic and had a professional degree. I set him up with Devorah, a smart, beautiful, educated, *baalas teshuva*. They hit it off immediately and after seven dates he asked her to marry, and she agreed. A few months after the wedding they moved back to the States and Yosef started working. They had a baby boy after a year, and everything seemed to be going well.

I happened to be in the States when I got a frantic call from Devorah. She was very angry.

"How could you do this to me?" she screamed.

I had no idea what she was talking about.

"You never told me about his history of mental illness."

"What history?" I spoke. "What are you talking about?

"You never told me that he was manic-depressive and was even taking medication for it."

I told her, "I never knew he had mental health problems or was manic-depressive."

"I don't believe you. You lied to me."

"I'm really sorry, but I never heard about this until just

now."

"You didn't know he was on lithium? Don't you ask about physical and mental health?" she cried.

"I do. All he told me was that when he was in Medical School, he was having difficulties concentrating on his studies and went to a psychiatrist who prescribed some medication to help him concentrate."

"I don't believe you. You've ruined my life."

"What exactly is the problem?" I asked.

"Well, he stopped taking his medication and quit his job at the hospital. He sits in front of the computer screen all day watching salacious sites. He's stopped learning and isn't religious anymore. Is that enough?"

"Wow, I'm really sorry, I had no idea."

"I don't believe you," she said.

I really didn't know what to say or do after that tongue-lashing but resolved to be more vigilant about mental health issues in the future. They got divorced.

Years later, I heard that Devorah had gotten remarried to a nice religious guy and was very happy. I also saw Yosef a couple of years after that. He wasn't religious and he seemed to be both manic-depressive and paranoid schizophrenic. I had failed. But *Hashem* had straightened out the accounts, at least for Devorah.

Shortly after that call from Devorah, Rafael came to me for a *shidduch*. He told me that he moved to Israel from Canada, where he was the CEO of a publicly traded tech company, five years before. He also told me that he had a PhD from UCLA in Psychology and had a thriving therapeutic practice in Jerusalem. He seemed dynamic and funny and extremely self-confident. I had seen his name on posters around town advertising his many seminars on self-improvement.

The first question I always asked was the interviewee's birth date. Since many older singles lie about their age, in asking for a birth date, which everyone knows, I would probably notice hesitancy in the answer if some were to lie.

"So, Rafael, what's your date of birth?"

"I'm twenty-eight," he responded.

"I asked you for a date of birth, not your age."

He hesitated, as if calculating the year, and answered appropriately.

He looked much older to me, but sometimes looks are deceiving.

"Wow... So, when did you get your PhD?"

"When I was twenty."

"That's very young," I said.

"I was in a big hurry to get on with my life, so I worked really hard."

"Let me get this straight," I said. "It takes a minimum of three or four years to get a PhD after a master's. That means you started college at thirteen or fourteen?"

"Yes. That's right."

"An amazing feat. And on top of that, you rose to be the CEO of a major Canadian company before you moved to Israel five years ago?"

"Yes."

"How was that possible? It means that you were twenty-three when you left Canada and had been the CEO before that?"

"I worked while I was getting my PhD."

This sounded far-fetched, especially since the he claimed that company was in Vancouver and he was studying at UCLA.

We continued with the interview, and I told Rafael at the

end that I'd get back to him with suggestions if I had any.

After he left, I started searching the Internet to see if I could find him there. I couldn't find any PhD graduates from UCLA in Psychology with his name in the year he mentioned or any other year near to that one. I also couldn't find his name as the CEO of the Canadian company he mentioned. I also wrote to UCLA to ask if they ever had a student enrolled in their school with his name. I called him the next day.

"Rafael. I couldn't find your name as having received a PhD from UCLA in that year or any other."

Without hesitation, he answered, "That's because I changed my name from my original name to my present one shortly after I graduated."

"Well, what was your original name?"

"I can't pronounce it. It brings back too many painful memories."

"What do you mean?"

"I ran away from my home in Omaha when I was fourteen. I couldn't stand my parents' abuse any more. I hitchhiked to LA and was homeless and then I decided I needed to make something of myself and enrolled in UCLA."

"How did they accept you? You didn't have a high school diploma."

"They tested me and saw that my IQ was 'off the charts' and took me in with a full scholarship."

"I see." I knew that I was dealing with a pathological liar.

"So, you won't be able to check me out on the Internet, except under my present name."

Rafael was a good liar, but not a great one, and sounded as phony as a three-dollar bill. I wouldn't set him up.

I later heard that he was arrested for rape and fraud. He

charged his "patients" for his therapy, but he actually had no license or any degrees. And his preferred method of therapy for his female clients was a twisted version of regression therapy, in which they would "visualize" everything that happened to them from conception to the present. To aid them he would be an active participant in the earliest phase of that playback.

The moral of this story is that deception runs deep in the human psyche, and as with anything else, in *shidduchim* the rule is: "let the buyer beware".

I almost never got involved in either the *Yeshiva* or *Chassidishe* Worlds of *shidduchim*. My area of expertise was almost exclusively with *baalei teshuva* or converts, which is quite different, as illustrated above.

CHAPTER XX
My Career as a *Shadchan*

By the time I arrived in Israel in 1986, there were perhaps a thousand foreign, unmarried, young English-speaking men who were studying in *Yeshivos* in Israel. There were at least as many foreign, unmarried, young English-speaking women seminary students. The *baal teshuva* phenomenon had also swept Israeli society, especially in the exciting aftermath of the Six Day War, with the recapture of the Old City of Jerusalem and the Temple Mount. Many secular soldiers were so moved by the seeming miraculous nature of the War that they were ripe for the message of our ancient and everlasting faith. *Yeshivot* for Israelis without religious backgrounds soon opened. They all needed to get married.

The day after I agreed to Rabbi Schmidt's offer, my phone started ringing off the hook with calls from the Nof girls. And as I interviewed more young women, I began interviewing more young *yeshiva* men. I scheduled two interviews an evening. Each took about an hour. They came to my home for the interview, and I typed their answers into files on my computer. I also took digital photos to attach to their files. As I was soon to learn, I was the first *shadchan* to use computer technology. Everyone else, it seemed, wrote their notes in longhand. This was not surprising since most *shadchanim* were older women who were unfamiliar with computers. The computer allowed me to add notes and comments after the initial interview without having to write in microscopic handwriting in the margins of a notebook. I could now search using keywords, which made the process more efficient. It helped that I had taken a course in personal typing in high school.

I began the interview by engaging in light conversation. I asked how difficult it was to find our apartment (it's difficult because of an irrational numbering system of both the buildings in our neighborhood and the apartments in our building); how long it took them to get here; where they were from and what life was like back home. I made a quick note of physical characteristics, their Jewish, religious, family, and educational backgrounds and then asked the interviewees to describe themselves.

This part of the interview was extremely important. While I picked up on tics, body language and speech patterns, I didn't know the person sitting in front of me, so I asked them what they thought would describe them best. Some would tell me what others said about them—that they are this way or that. I would tell them:

"I don't care what others think of you, I want to know what you think of yourself."

For many this was a very difficult question. Most of the interviewees were quite young—between nineteen and twenty-four. It's not an age when one is overly introspective. Many young men and women have a poor self-image, but that's not the same as introspection. They only see themselves as compared to the false and exaggerated images they have of popular peers and find themselves wanting. This has only been magnified by social media, where almost everyone lies about the "thrilling" lives they lead.

As a person matures, they should be developing a strong

self-image. As they reach marriageable age, they realize that they must sell themselves to the *shadchan* as one sells himself or herself to a potential employer. At least those were mostly the ones I saw. I imagine that there were several young singles whose self-image was so poor that they didn't think of themselves as marriageable material and whom I never met. When someone would hesitate to describe themself in a positive way, I would say to them, "you forgot to mention that you're very modest." (Which reminds me of a joke I once heard, "Do you know Joe Schmo? He's very modest." "Yes," responds his friend, "and he has a lot to be modest about.").

Mostly I heard the same adjectives used: "searching, spiritual, kind, and trustworthy." At some point I would say, "I used to be in the Boy Scouts too, let me add the other adjectives in the Scout's creed: "helpful, courteous, reverent, etc., etc." I was trying to get something more unique out of their descriptions and would ask leading questions like: "You say you're kind. What do you do to show that kindness? How many times a week, a month, a year? How are your relations with your parents and siblings? Your roommates? What do you think is your best quality… your worst?"

I would ask about their hobbies or what they enjoy doing in their spare time. For those who answered that they had no spare time (mostly guys who were learning in *yeshiva*) I would ask what they would like to do if they had spare time.

The next question was, what plans did they have for the future? This was a tricky one. As I described in my daughter Miriam's high school education, the prevailing line from their teachers was the idealistic objective of working to support their husbands and families, while also bearing and bringing up large numbers of children. Although such a plan was almost entirely unrealistic, many of the younger women in *baalei teshuva* seminaries were convinced that they could pull it off. How they would do this was a bit of a mystery to themselves, but they would trust that *Hashem* would provide—an admirable attitude, albeit a bit naive. Single women, over twenty-five, were more realistic and while generally willing to work for a year or two to support their husbands in learning, they wanted to be able to stay at home and raise a family. They needed a guy who had a realistic plan to make a living.

Most of the guys I met wanted to learn as long as possible and then work. They had college degrees, and some were professionals. They were confident of their futures. There were some, of course, who only wanted to learn.

I also asked if they planned to live in Israel.

The final question was, what they were looking for in a spouse? The answers were mostly predictable. Guys wanted girls who were slim. That was, hands down, the most common request. After that, they wanted a girl who was pretty, well mannered, polite, healthy, and fit. They all wanted someone who was at their religious level—usually *charedie*. Also, someone who liked children and was a good housekeeper.

Occasionally, the requirements were weird. I remember one guy who apart from all the usual requirements also wanted a wife who was highly intelligent, had at least one graduate degree, and who hung the toilet paper facing out, not toward the wall. He had many other extremely detailed requirements, but that last one was the one that stood out. After I finished the interview, he asked me if I had anyone for him. I told him I didn't at the time, but if something came up, I'd call. A week later he called me to ask if I had found someone. I hadn't. I was frankly afraid to set him up with anyone who might be sensitive—to being micromanaged by a despotic and controlling husband, which was probably every woman in the world. He had told me that he was a computer programmer. Now he told me that he was an expert hacker and if I didn't come up with a suggestion in three days he was going to hack into my computer and look for himself. I had no idea how he was going to do that since at that time I wasn't connected to the Internet, but I assumed that he might be capable of anything. I didn't set him up and after a few more months he left me alone.

After completing the interview I'd ask for two or three references and their contact information and then take their digital photo. In the case of a woman who had never been married, I'd ask her if she could marry a *Cohen. Cohanim,* the priestly class, cannot marry divorced women, converts, or one who had relations with a non-Jew. I was always uncomfortable asking this question, but it was necessary.

I'd then search my files for an appropriate match. My method was not computer matching. I only used the computer to search for appropriate age, willingness to live in Israel or outside of Israel and suitability for a *Cohen*, if the guy happened to be one.

I would describe my method of matchmaking as getting a certain "vibe" from the people sitting in front of me. While I believe I was always the beneficiary of *"siyata d'Shmaya"*— help from Heaven, on occasion I saw it in bold relief.

A case of the latter occurred as I was finishing my interview with Melody, a twenty-seven-year-old English woman. She was an Oxford graduate with an Oxford MBA. She had been a vice president at Goldman Sachs in London when she decided to become religious and study at the Nof Yerushalayim Women's Seminary. Not surprisingly, she wanted someone with at least a university degree and, preferably, an intellectual and a professional. I knew I was going to have a hard time matching her up with someone who was equally brilliant, educated, and self-confident. Soon after the end of the interview, as I was scrolling through my files for an appropriate match, I got a call from a guy who had recently been to see me for a *shidduch*. I knew Chaim very well. He had been a frequent *Shabbos* guest at our table, and he was studying at Ohr HaTzadikim because my friend Eliot, a lawyer in Detroit, directed Chaim to me. Before he started his journey to *Torah* and *Mitzvot*, Chaim had worked for Eliot as a cleaner in his office. Chaim was a secular Israeli, who had dropped out of high school at seventeen and joined the Army. After his three-year service he, like so many other ex-Israeli soldiers, traveled to India and the Far East to recapture, with a vengeance, a missed wild and abandoned youth. He ended up in Detroit where he hoped to make a pile of money before returning home. Unfortunately, without any higher education and no particular skills, the only employment he found was doing odd jobs like cleaning offices. He was barely making enough to live on and going nowhere fast. Chaim loved the Shabbos meals at Eliot's home and then became interested in the Torah classes given at the local *shul*. Eliot convinced him to come to *Yeshiva*.

After more than 70 years on this earth, I have come to certain conclusions. One of them is that the world is composed of basically two levels of intelligent people. One, which we call genius, is almost immediately recognizable to anyone who has encountered it. I would describe it as an almost immediate grasp of the most esoteric, disparate, and complex facts and ideas, and the ability to instantaneously synthesize them into a cohesive and ordered whole and to defend those conclusions against rational and intelligent attack. Then there are the rest of us. We can learn things, even very complex things, and develop sophisticated ideas and conclusions, if we are so motivated, but not in a flash. I didn't think Chaim was a genius but despite his lack of secular education, he was very intelligent and, being motivated, became an exceptional learner in the *Yeshiva*.

I took his phone call as a sign from Heaven. Maybe this was a match? This wholly illogical thought was part and parcel of my matchmaking process. I would get a "feeling" about a match or see a "sign" and proceed.

I said to Melody, "Forgive me. This is going to sound a bit bizarre, but the guy who just called me might be a possible *shidduch* for you. He dropped out of high school, never went to college and worked as a menial laborer. But I know him well and he's highly intelligent, an excellent learner, a deep thinker, and a hard worker. It could be *hashgacha pratis* (Divine Providence) that Chaim called as I was interviewing you. I think it might be worth one date."

I forgot to mention that Chaim was very athletic and exceedingly good looking. That helped. Melody met him and was swept off her feet. All of a sudden, his lack of formal education wasn't so important. She had enough for both. His plan was to become a rabbi and teach. That was good enough for her and he didn't feel threatened by her. After six dates he proposed. They were happily married.

Another example of visible *siyata d'Shemaya* was a *shidduch* my wife suggested for a single friend of mine. Yisroel was an English, keyboard-playing, rock musician who had some professional success in his home country, Europe, and the United States. His band recorded a platinum album. He later became a producer for a major record label. He was about my age (around forty) at the time and never married. Valerie was a young Mexican woman who was fifteen years his junior. She had been a *prima ballerina* in the Mexico City Ballet Company. When her father died, she came to Israel to explore her Jewish roots. We met Valerie through the well-known *kiruv* worker, Rabbi Meyer Schuster, who sent her to our house for a *Shabbos* meal. We brought her to a Latin American women's seminary in the area and she flourished there. She was a frequent guest at our home. After about six months, my wife suggested that we set her up with Yisroel. I thought the idea was preposterous. She spoke no English—only Spanish. He spoke no Spanish—only English. He was almost old enough to be her father. But my wife insisted, saying that we had nothing to lose by setting them up. My wife told me that she had spoken to Valerie, and she was fine with the idea. I spoke to Yisroel, who was skeptical, but willing.

After their first date I asked him how they communicated. "Mostly with gestures and very poor Hebrew," he answered. She liked him and wanted to go out again. He was game. She liked him even more after the second date. But the impracticalities of the *shidduch* seemed to create an unbridgeable gap. How can one have a meaningful relationship without being able to communicate? Valerie had taken a couple of years of English in high school, but wasn't interested at that time, and had learned almost nothing. Now she decided that she was going to learn English fast. After five weeks, she spoke passable English and language was no longer an obstacle. They married and, *bli eyin hara,* have raised a large family in Jerusalem—proving again that ideas for successful *shidduchim* are obviously inspired from above, and not necessarily logical.

I have made, *Boruch Hashem,* over seventy *shidduchim* in

the years that I was active. Very few of them were *obviously* a result of *siyata d'Shemaya,* although I'm sure all of them were. I worked quite hard at my profession, often spending five or six hours a day on *shidduchim.* Most of my work involved getting my clients to examine themselves and recognize their own motives, strengths, and weaknesses, and to give others the benefit of the doubt.

At the beginning of the process, I would set up the date myself. I didn't want the couple to speak on the phone (as is common in *shidduchim* in America). It is quite awkward for a guy to ask a girl, whom he has never met before, for a date—even if she knows that he'll be calling. Not every guy is talented at "breaking the ice" on a phone call. Many lack self-confidence and a girl could get a very negative impression before they even meet. Also, the guy or girl might reflect on the call, kick themselves for saying this or for not saying that, and conclude that he or she sounded stupid and that the other would never consider them seriously as a match. I wanted to avoid that.

I would pick the location of the date and tell the guy to be dressed and groomed to look his best. The girls didn't need my advice in that regard. First meetings were usually at hotel lobbies with a beverage service. I would describe the parties to each other and the exact location in the lobby where they should meet. At first, I didn't think this would be a problem, but after a few cases of mistaken identity—where a guy approached the wrong girl—I decided that the girl should tell me something distinctive that she would be wearing or carrying so he could easily identify her. Even with these signs it happened that, in at least one instance, the guy approached the wrong girl, who had the same name as his intended date and began the conversion until her *shidduch* appeared.

I coached the parties on the conversations to have on each date; how long the date should last; what to order; how to dress; how to speak; and how to act. Since almost all my clients were *baalei teshuva* and had never dated in a religious setting, they needed to know the rules. Touching was absolutely forbidden. Overt flirting was out of the question. Certain subjects were off limits. This was a new world to them.

The next day I would spend hours with each person, analyzing the date. From my experience I gleaned certain tendencies—nothing earthshaking, but valuable to me. Many guys would tell me: "I knew in the first fifteen seconds that she wasn't right for me." This usually meant that he didn't find her attractive enough. I knew viscerally that this was a huge mistake. How so? Once a girl from Nof, named Nechama, came for an interview. She was a PhD student in Psychology at a top university in the States, who had taken a year off to study at Nof. When I first saw Nechama, I was struck by the fact that she looked very much like my sister, whom I consider very attractive. I set her up with Adam who was particular about looks. I told him before they met that she was slim and quite attractive. After their date she told me that she'd be interested in going out again, but he told me that while she was interesting to talk to, she wasn't for him and didn't want another date.

"What was the problem? "I asked.

"I wasn't attracted. She wasn't very pretty."

I was personally offended and said to him, "Adam, go out with her again. She happens to be objectively attractive. In fact, she looks just like my sister."

I suppose, for fear of offending me, he agreed to go out again. Surprisingly after his second date he saw her in a different light and thought that she was attractive.

Attractiveness, for women, as I've learnt over the years, has more to do with personality than looks. For men, it's also true, but they don't realize it. A woman's manner of speaking or kindness or modesty can be attractive to a man, but he'll tend to translate that into looks.

Sometimes I would set up a girl who I thought was very plain looking, but an interesting conversationalist, and the guy would come back from the date and when I asked what they spoke about, he told me he couldn't remember because he was so blinded by her beauty.

While many guys are superficial when it comes to dating preferences, it doesn't mean they are uneducable. They simply must be taught to think more deeply before deciding solely based on a first impression.

To that end I would almost always insist on a second date if the girl was interested. Unless the guy was impervious to my many arguments, he usually would agree.

Of course, the opposite was also true. Because guys heard from their *rabbeim* that the most important qualities in a potential mate is her modesty, her religiosity, her ability to manage a household and support her husband, many had the idea that attractiveness was not only unimportant, but, against Torah values. After all, King Solomon wrote: "Charm is false and beauty is worthless, but a woman who fears G-d, she shall be praised...." (*Proverbs* Chapter 31). While Solomon's words are true, (after all, with 1000 wives, he knew something about women), I believe most men must be physically attracted to their wives. If not, the marriage probably will not be successful.

In interviewing divorced *baalei teshuva* men, I discovered that one of the main reasons for the divorce was that they had assumed or had read that a *shidduch* should only be made with a *tzaddekas*—a righteous woman, regardless of her looks. In biographies about *gedolim*—great religious figures, the *Rosh HaYeshiva* would approach the young *bochur* with the most potential for greatness in learning in the *yeshiva* and offer him a *shidduch* with his daughter. Looks were never a factor, and no one would ever refuse. The offer was usually accompanied with a job as a *rebbe* in the *yeshiva* and the potential of becoming the *Rosh HaYeshiva* one day. Of course, this had nothing to do with Cameron (now known as Kalman) who until two years ago didn't know a pair of *tzitzit* from a pair of pliers and whose main pursuit at college was chasing girls.

After reporting back to me about the date, if a guy said, "I'd like to go out with her again." I would ask, "What did you like about her?"

If he didn't say anything about attractiveness, I'd ask him about it. If he said he didn't think she was attractive, but that shouldn't matter to him, I knew that unless he felt some attraction after the next one or two dates, I'd have to pull the plug. I would tell him that it's important that he finds his future wife attractive, and we'll see if that will change after the next date or two.

I coached them on the conversations they should be having at different stages in the dating process. The theme of the first date should be getting to know the other party. One shouldn't discuss weighty matters or future life plans. The date shouldn't be longer than an hour and a half and no shorter than an hour. Less than that, he would risk offending the young woman and more than that he would risk boring her to death.

The best advice for that first date is to stick to the Three F's—Food, Family and "Filosophy." I had heard this from one of my *rebbeim*, Rabbi Moshe Carlebach (may he have a *refuah shelaima*—a complete recovery). And he would joke, that if she answers by saying that she's orphaned, an only child, not particularly fond of food and never thought about philosophy, you could cover the three by asking her: "But, if you had a brother would he like *lukshon* (noodles)?"

The following is not a real case, but a composite of many real dates. It serves as a model of what not to do on a first date.

Avraham and Rochel (formerly known as Andrew and Roxanne) meet at the Jerusalem Gate Hotel. The date was called for 8:00 p.m. and at 8:07 I get a call from Rochel.

"Rabbi Semenow?"

"Speaking."

"Where's Avraham?"

"He's probably stuck in traffic. Let me call him and get back to you."

I call Avraham on his cell phone. He answers.

"Avraham, it's 8:10 p.m. Your date was called for eight p.m. What happened to you?"

"We finished *davening maariv* at the *yeshiva* a little later than usual. I didn't get out until five to eight."

"That's totally irresponsible," I tell him. "You know what they say… 'You never get a second chance to make a first impression…' If you get a second date, promise me that you'll either *daven maariv* at an earlier *minyan* or after your date. I want you to be at the date at least ten minutes earlier than the set time. You do want to get married, don't you?"

"Yes."

"Promise me?"

"I promise."

"How long will it take you to get to the hotel?"

"Ten minutes or so."

"Okay then, I'll cover for you this time, but never do this again."

I call Rochel back.

"I'm terribly sorry," I tell her. "It's totally my fault. I told him that the date was set for 8:30 p.m. He'll be there soon."

At this point, I enter in my notes that I covered for him and he's not punctual and might be irresponsible.

Later that evening, I hear about the date.

The first person to call me is Rochel.

Women are so good with words. I don't have to pull teeth to get the details of the date.

"Can I be honest with you?" says Rochel.

"Please don't," I say, "I hate it when people tell me the truth, I'd much rather that you lie to me." (I don't know why I say things like that so often. It must be because I spent so much of my youth watching comedy teams like Laurel and Hardy and Abbott and Costello. I keep forgetting that young people don't know when I'm being sarcastic). I quickly add, "Just joking. Please tell me exactly what happened. Just the facts, ma'am. Just the facts." (There I go again with a Detective Joe Friday impersonation).

"Well, as you know, I'd been waiting for him for over a half hour and sitting there in the lobby all alone and the waitress kept coming over to me from time to time asking me if I wanted to order, I felt uncomfortable."

"Very understandably," I commiserated.

"I mean, I knew it wasn't his fault. You had given him a different time, but still I was uncomfortable."

"Yes."

"When he came into the lobby, he looked a bit unkempt.

His shirt was untucked, his tie was askew, his hat was pushed to the back of his head, and he was sweating. It looked like he had run from Har Nof (where his *yeshiva* was located) to the hotel. He did invite me to have a drink but nothing to eat. I ordered Pepsi. Not that I would have accepted a piece of cake, but it would have been nice had he asked."

"What did you talk about?"

"He started by asking me about my family. I told him that I was the oldest of three and my parents were both working professionals. He then started telling me about his own family. He doesn't really get along with his siblings. He's a middle child and felt neglected by his parents. When he became religious, his parents saw it as a rebellion against them and weren't happy with his demands that they keep *kosher* and *Shabbos*. He wanted nothing more to do with them. He hasn't spoken to them in the last year. He was trying to convince his younger brother to become religious but hasn't had any success. He loves his *yeshiva* and wants to learn for as long as possible. In fact, after his initial question, he only talked about himself. He didn't seem interested in me at all. He also seemed quite angry, and I'm concerned about his lack of tolerance for his non-religious family. That could be an indication that he has anger, patience, and tolerance issues that might play out in a marriage. He also doesn't have a plan to make a living. I want a husband who'll work after a year or two. I don't want to go out with him again."

Rochel's analysis seemed to be very perceptive. I hadn't noticed much of what she said in my interview with Avraham.

When I interviewed him, Avraham told me that he got along very well with his family. I should have been more probing, and I added to my list of questions: "When was the last time you spoke to your parents?" If the answer was "not in the last few months," I'd ask, "why not?"

Avraham called me the next evening.

"Why didn't you call me last night, after the date?" I asked.

"I was busy with other things. I thought it would be OK."

"Next time, call me after the date if it's before 11 p.m. So, what did you think?"

"I thought she was nice. I'd like to go out again."

"Tell me about the date?"

"Well, as you already know, I got there late and apologized for that. She was attractive and a good listener."

"Did you ask her any questions?"

"I asked about her family and school."

"What did you ask her after that?"

"You know, the usual stuff."

"Like what?"

"I can't remember."

"Did you hear from her?" he asked anxiously. "Does she want to go out again?"

"I did hear from her. She wanted to consult with her *rebbetzin* at the seminary before she got back to me about a second date."

Even though I knew she didn't want a second date, I didn't want to hurt his feelings. I wanted him to think that she was considering the possibility of a second date.

I called him back the next day.

"I'm sorry, Avraham, Rochel decided not to go out again."

"Did she give you a reason?"

"Yes. She told me that you looked disheveled when you arrived. You didn't offer her anything to eat. You seemed to ignore her and talk almost exclusively about yourself."

Avraham paused a few seconds before answering me. "I guess I messed up badly."

"Yes."

"I was very nervous and worried about gaps in the conversation. I guess I got carried away."

"Sounds like that."

"Did she say anything else?"

"Yes. She said that despite that, you seemed like a very nice guy, but she wanted someone who has a plan for a *parnassa (livelihood)*—not a guy who plans to 'learn as long as possible.' She doesn't want to support her husband forever."

Now, while she didn't say she thought him to be a very nice guy, I thought I'd add that because I didn't want him to feel like a complete failure. He would need some self-confidence for his next date.

In the meantime, I had my work cut out for me with Avraham.

Over the next hour, I dissected the date and their conversation with a sharp scalpel. I emphasized again how important it is to be punctual. How he had to pay more attention to his date and make her the focus of the conversation. If she had any questions about him, he should answer them completely and honestly and not add extraneous emotions or editorial comments. The time to show his emotional side is better left for a later date.

I told him that he should have offered her something to eat and drink and how important it was to be gracious and to show that he was sincere in his request. I then told him that Rochel mentioned that he seemed to have some anger issues with his family. I asked him to explore them with me.

"Is it true that you don't have a good relationship with your family?"

"Yes."

"Did you have a happy childhood?"

"Yeah. Pretty normal and happy until I was eleven when my folks divorced, and I went to live with my mom. She got married soon after the divorce and I didn't get along with my stepdad. He was cold and stingy."

"Was he Jewish?"

"No. But neither was my birth father."

This is an increasingly common phenomenon that I have noticed in the applications that come into the *Yeshiva*. I often joke that if the guy's last name is O'Toole, he's probably Jewish, since a person's status as a Jew is determined by matrilineal descent, but if his name is Goldberg we must check to see if his mother is Jewish.

"How was the relationship affected after you became religious?"

"I realize now that I was suffering from a "recent *baal teshuva* syndrome." I was so convinced that I had found the Truth that anyone who was not equally convinced was a heretic and had to be warned about the error of their ways. Of course, the fact that my dad and stepdad are both *goyim* only made me crazier. I mean even though I'm a full Jew, I'm still half *goy*."

Avraham had indeed put his finger on a shared attitude among recent converts to all faiths. There is an intolerance of those who are not like-minded. *Baalei Teshuva,* although not converts, share with them the fact that before they weren't believers and now, they are. Many are genuinely worried about their family's place in Heaven. Many are just as intolerant as they were before they "got religion" but now have a righteous moral perch to be intolerant from. Avraham had to be taught that the Torah tells us to "honor your parents"—regardless of their level of observance. The only time when he can disobey them is when they tell him to do something opposite to one of the commandments in the Torah. I told him that honoring them means to speak to them respectfully and politely. And that even includes his stepfather. I suggested that he call his parents in the next day or two and let me know that he did and tell me about the call. He should inquire about their welfare and their health and tell them about his life. Avraham said he would do so. And he did.

Sometimes people surprise me. Ari was a very quiet and studious *bochur* in the *Yeshiva*. One would not say he was outstanding in any way, except in terms of his determination. He seemed determined to do the right thing in every situation—which is, in a way, exceptional. He was approaching twenty-six and decided it was time for him to get married. I was acquainted with him but didn't know him well. He certainly didn't strike me as a go-getter in anything but learning. I was wrong. When it came time for him to date, he was singular in his focus. He told me he had prepared for dating by reading a book written by a rabbi on the subject. I had also read that book and thought it offered good advice. But reading advice in a book and following it are often two very different things.

I fixed Ari up with Leah. Leah was a fun-loving and very smart young woman who had gone to an Ivy League school and then earned an MBA at MIT. She was studying at Nof Yerushalayim and was determined to marry a *talmid chacham* and support him. When I was interviewing her and going through my list of guys, I came across Ari's name. I hesitated. On one hand Ari was a guy of modest ability in learning and probably not as bright as Leah, but, on the other, he was very serious about learning and given his record so far, seemed to have the determination to learn full time for many years. I remembered something that I heard about Rav Moshe Feinstein, *z'l*, the greatest *poseik* (*halachic* authority) in America. Some rabbi who was in *yeshiva* with him in Europe said that Rav Moshe was an average *bochur*, but what distinguished him was his *hasmada*—his dedication and willingness to put in long hours in his quest to master the Torah. After years of intense learning, he became Rav Moshe, one of the *gedolei hador*.

Of course, in Europe, only those *bochurim* of outstanding ability went to *yeshiva* after *bar mitzvah*. Almost everyone else went to work to help support his family. So, the fact that Rav Moshe was in *yeshiva* meant that he was outstanding. According to that rabbi telling the story, he might have been average for the *yeshiva*, but that's like saying he was average for a physics major at Cambridge. But, then again, I thought, who knows, maybe Dovid will also turn out to be a *godol*. I suggested his name to Leah, with all my caveats. He didn't seem to have much of a sense of humor, he was quiet and reserved and had gone to a community college for a year before he came to *yeshiva*; but he was determined and intelligent and wanted to learn. She agreed to the *shidduch* and they went out.

The next day I heard from both of them, and both seemed pleased with the date. I asked Dovid what they spoke about. He told me that the book said to talk about family, school, and the girl—the author's version of the Three F's I mentioned above. He did that. The date lasted one and half-hours to the minute, which was also according to the book. On their second date he gave her a small book of *Tehillim* (Psalms), inexpensive, but thoughtful, and thanked her for agreeing to see him for a second date. She was very impressed (she hadn't read that book). They discussed family and their plans. On their third date he complimented her by telling her she looked very nice and that her dress was very becoming. This was all according to the book. He wouldn't have had the temerity to say such a thing if the author didn't suggest it. Their fourth date was a day trip to a park in town with a picnic—it was springtime. He also gave her a silver necklace with her name spelled out in Hebrew. The fifth was an invitation to dinner at a fine restaurant. This was already very serious. The sixth date was the proposal. She accepted. He did it by the book and it worked. I was impressed. I told him that now he had to read a book on marriage. With a wry smile, he told me that he already had.

They married, and after a year, a friend of hers, who was making and selling jewelry in the Old City of Jerusalem, was having a difficult time managing her business. She was very good as a designer and artist but knew nothing about business and was losing money. She asked Leah to help her. Using her knowledge gained in business school she transformed the artist's studio into a showroom and began to sell online. Today the business is thriving and can support not just Leah's and her friend's families, but also those of their many employees. Ari is still learning and has published several *seforim (*religious texts).

I worked in *shiddhuchim f*or close to fifteen years. The work was satisfying but very time consuming. As my responsibilities in the *Yeshiva* increased, I had much less time to devote to it. Also, I wasn't getting the same "*geshmacht*" (enjoyment) from the process and as a result, was making far fewer matches than I did in my early years. It was time to stop.

Now I had more time to do other things. Like writing this book.

That's not entirely true. I stopped doing *shidduchim* as a

career in 2015 and have made a few since, *Boruch Hashem*. I only started this book during the Pandemic of 2020. I guess you could say this is one of the upsides of Covid—or not—if you don't enjoy the book. Of course, if that was the case why are you still reading it?

CHAPTER XXI
Lying vs. Changing the Narrative

You might question my behavior in the retelling or inventing certain scenarios—like covering for Avraham's tardiness by telling Rochel that I mistakenly gave Avraham the wrong time for the date. Or when I told Avraham that Rochel thought he was a very nice guy.

The Torah says *"m'dvar sheker tirchok"*—keep far away from a lie. So, wasn't I violating a commandment written in the Holy Torah?

We have three Patriarchs: Avraham, Yitzchok and Yaacov. Our tradition tells us that Avraham endowed his progeny with kindness; Yitzchok, with uncompromising service to our Creator; and Yaacov—with Truth. The *Gemara* also says that Truth is the "signature of the Creator". It is also the foundation of the Torah, which we call *Toras Emes*—the True Torah.

So, how could I lie? The answer is, I didn't.

The *Midrash* recounts that prior to *Hashem's* creating Man, He opened the idea to discussion before the Heavenly Court of Angels. There was a huge argument. The Angel of *Chesed* (Kindness) thought it was a great idea because of all the acts of loving kindness to be performed by Man. The Angel of *Emes* (Truth) said: "don't create him, because men will constantly lie." The Angel of *Tzedek* (Righteousness) advocated for Man's creation because men will establish a just legal system. Lastly, the Angel of *Shalom* (Peace) cast his "no" vote because men would constantly fight. There will be wars and conflict, murder, and mayhem. The vote was now two against two. How did *Hashem* resolve the draw? He threw *Emes* to Earth. When questioned by the remaining angels how He could do such a thing? He answered: "Let Truth spring from the Earth." (*Bereshis Rabba* 8:8).

Questions abound. Firstly, why would Hashem open for discussion the topic of creating Man? Would their discussions have any bearing on His decision? Secondly, do angels have free will? Can they have opinions? Aren't they just messengers of Hashem? The answer is: The *Midrash* isn't recounting an actual event. It's just illustrating to us, in a form that we can understand, the variables that Hashem considered before creating Man.

You might also ask; how could these Angels know what Man would do if he hadn't yet been created? The answer is that *Hashem* and his Angels don't live in a time bound universe. Present, past and future are all revealed. "Okay," you might say, "but if the outcome is known, what's the point of creating Man? The history of every person who has ever lived or will ever live is an open book to Hashem. He knows exactly how a person will act before the person himself knows. And if that's true, where is free will?"

This is a good question and one that our greatest philosophers have grappled with throughout the ages and no answer is really satisfying—at least not to me. But that's okay. I recognize my limited ability to comprehend such esoteric questions, so I'll just take it on faith that there's an answer. It doesn't really bother me that I'll never know it in my lifetime. There are plenty of things in the universe that I don't understand—like Einstein's Theory of Relativity, but I take it on faith that it's very brilliant and probably true.

When the *Medrash* says that *Hashem* threw *Emes* down to Earth, it has two possible interpretations:

1. That *Hashem* was "angry" at Truth for being so negative and wanted to cancel his vote, so he threw him out of court; or

2. That *Hashem* wanted Truth to reside on Earth because it was important that Man seek and find the Truth.

In the Heavenly Ivory Tower, so to speak, Truth looks at things in a pure way. Something is true or false—one and one is two. No one could argue that it's really three. But once Truth takes up residence on Earth, things are not so clear. While one and one might be unquestionably two, when two travelers are dying of thirst in the desert and one has a canteen with just enough water so that if he drinks it himself, he might live long enough to get to an oasis, but if he shares it with his friend, they'll both die—that's a question that Truth on Earth might think twice or even thrice about. At the conclusion of many debates the Talmud states: *"Eilu v'eilu divrei Elokim Chaim"*— "both opinions are True and are the Words of the Living G-d." That's why the Sages said: "there are seventy facets to the Torah"—seventy ways of looking at Truth. Each one sees the same object but because they look from their own perspective, which is never the same as the perspective of his neighbor, it looks somewhat different, but it's all true.

The Angel of *Emes* was right. People don't always tell the truth. I might modify that statement to say that all normal people lie. I have heard that some people with Asperger's syndrome cannot tolerate an untruth. While the rest of us might feel comfortable entertaining or even speaking the occasional lie or exaggeration, people like Greta Thunberg, probably today's most famous Asperger's sufferer, cannot. Everyone in the world must admit that climate change is a death knell to our life on this planet and pledge to do all they can to change our behaviors to minimize our footprint or endure her constant harping. She probably cannot tolerate a comment like: "It's a lovely day today." The speaker must acknowledge that it's a terrible day because the world is coming to an end. It must be really hard on her parents!

Lying began at the beginning of Creation, in the Garden of Eden. *Adom* (Adam), the first man, was commanded not to eat from The Tree of Knowledge of Good and Evil, and that if he did, he would bring Death into the World. From *Chava's* (Eve's) subsequent conversation with the Serpent, it appears that *Adom* had told his wife that G-d had commanded them that they could neither "touch" the tree nor "eat" of it. He embellished on the one prohibition by adding a second one. That was the first lie. His motive, our Sages say, was to "put a fence around the Torah" as the Rabbis did later in history when they promulgated prohibitions to prevent people from violating various commandments in the Torah.

Examples of this abound. The way we Jews observe the Sabbath is almost entirely in conformity to Rabbinic Law. How we warm up food that has already been cooked, what objects we are allowed to touch, by what light we can read, these are all Rabbinic laws—to keep Jews from violating the Torah laws of the Sabbath. The difference between these prohibitions and *Adom's* is that the Rabbis clearly labeled their edicts as "Rabbinic law" and not Torah Law. In fact, one of the main objectives in discussions in Talmud is to determine what is Rabbinic and what is from the Torah.

Adom, however, failed to tell *Chava* that he had decided to add another prohibition to protect the first. The rabbis say: *"kol hamosif gorea"*—anyone who adds, takes away. *Adom* thought he was doing a good thing, but he was doing great harm. When the Serpent, who apparently knew what G-d had prohibited to *Adom*, asked *Chava* if there was anything that was prohibited to her and her husband, he already knew the answer. When she answered that they couldn't eat from the Tree of Knowledge or even touch it or they would die, he pushed her into the Tree and "proved" to her that just as she didn't die from touching it, she wouldn't die from eating it. And, in fact, she ate it and didn't die. She apparently was told by her husband that death would come immediately, although G-d told him no such thing. So, after touching the tree and remaining alive she could correctly surmise that eating from it would also not be harmful and maybe beneficial. After all, G-d had not spoken to her. As far as she knew, her husband invented the whole story for his own selfish purpose.

At that point the Serpent could have told her that there was no G-d and that she and her husband were just a product of a mutation after hundreds of millions of years of evolution. But he was smarter than that, because he knew that he could be proved wrong in the next few minutes when G-d spoke to *Adom* and *Chava*. Instead, he diminished G-d's stature by saying that He was jealous of Man. And that Man was almost co-equal to Him and that His reason for forbidding her husband from eating from the Tree was to prevent them from being co-equal Creators of the World. Thus, the Serpent sowed great doubt in her mind about the nature of the Creator. And it showed how the Serpent was, indeed, the cleverest being on earth. He took advantage of the simplicity and gullibility of Man.

Of course, *Adom* when being confronted by G-d with the

violation of his only commandment, dissimulated by saying, "Hey, it wasn't my fault, it was this woman who You gave to me. She convinced me to eat of the fruit" —implying that had she not been created; he would have remained pious. This was part of the Original Sin—*kofui tov*—ingratitude.

Later, *Yaacov Avinu* (our Father Jacob), tricks his brother *Eisav* (Esau) into selling him his birthright by taking advantage of his crazed state of hunger, and later, upon his mother's urging, "steals" the blessings meant for his brother by dressing up in *Eisav's* clothes and wearing hairy sleeves and neck covering and making believe that he, *Yaacov*, was his brother *Eisav*. This is the "Man of Truth!"

Eisav, soon afterwards, discovers his brother's deception, and vows to kill him. To save him himself from *Eisav's* murderous designs, *Yaacov* runs away to his uncle and future father-in-law, the wicked *Lavan* in *Aram Naharaim*. After twenty years, of being tricked and swindled by *Lavan*, both in *Yaacov's* marriages and his wages, he takes his family, flees from Lavan, and returns to the Land of Canaan, where he settles near the city of *Shechem*. When *Yaacov's* daughter, *Deena*, is raped and held captive by the prince of the city, *Yaacov's* sons, by means of subterfuge (more lying) kill all the men in *Shechem*.

Later *Yosef* (Joseph) is sold by his brothers into slavery in Egypt. The brothers implicitly lie to their father by sending *Yosef's* special coat of many colors dipped in the blood of a sheep to their father and asking him if he recognizes the coat. *Yaacov* draws his own conclusion that *Yosef* was attacked by a wild animal and eaten. His sons do not correct him. The charade was kept up for twenty-two years, and all the while their father was suffering from grief of a lost son and of the destruction of his family, all because they didn't tell the truth.

A drought and famine sweep across the Middle East. *Yaacov* sends his sons to Egypt to buy grain. Upon their return and after hearing a report of the brothers' encounter with the Viceroy (who unbeknownst to them was really *Yosef*) and the Viceroy's demand that they will be sold no more food in the future unless they are accompanied by *Binyamin*, Rochel's supposedly only surviving son, *Yaacov* asks them why they told the truth to the Viceroy about the number of children in their family and their welfare. He told them that they should have lied and not mention *Binyamin* at all.

And, of course, *Yosef*, by making believe that he was an Egyptian and mentally torturing his brothers with his many accusations, also lied.

At the end of the *Sefer Bereshis* (the Book of Genesis) after *Yaacov* is dead and buried, the brothers, fearing *Yosef's* wrath, lie to him, saying that their father had commanded them to tell Yosef that he, *Yaacov*, didn't want *Yosef* to hold a grudge against his brothers and that he should forgive them for their crime. *Rashi*, in his commentary, says that *Yaacov* said no such thing but that they were *"shina"* they varied the story for the purpose of peace.

So, from here we see that telling the Truth in every circumstance is not necessarily proper behavior. In fact, sometimes we should speak a falsehood to preserve or promote peace. If your wife bakes a cake and you don't really like it, but you tell her it's delicious, you are lying for the sake of peace. If your husband gets fired from his job and you tell him that he'll find a better one very soon, although you know that he's too old, not very skilled, and probably unemployable, you're lying for the sake of peace. What's the point of telling the truth? Why would you want to hurt his or her feelings for no good reason? These lies are sanctioned by the Torah.

We can, in retrospect, look at those instances when lies were appropriate and when they weren't. My point being that not every falsehood is an affront to Truth. It can just be an avoidance of conflict or a promotion of peace, which in the end is a service to Truth. So, I didn't "lie" to Avraham and Rochel, I just changed the narrative for the promotion of peace.

CHAPTER XXII
My Life as a *Schnorrer*

About nine months after I arrived at Ohr HaTzadikim, one of the *Roshei HaYeshiva*, Rav Gendelman, invited me to his office. He was the main fundraiser for the *Yeshiva* and asked me to consider going to Cleveland to collect donations from people I knew. Since I was one of the few students learning in the *Yeshiva* who had worked before coming to learn, I was somewhat uniquely qualified to help him raise funds. As a lawyer who had an active practice in Cleveland, I knew most of the businesspeople and professionals in the religious community. Also, as a young professional, I was asked to serve on the board of my *shul*, The Young Israel of Cleveland; I was an Officer and on the Board of Directors of the Telshe Yeshiva; and was President of Yavne Seminary. I was also active in the Jewish Federation of Cleveland, which served the wider Jewish Community. In those capacities, one of my main (sometimes only) functions was to give money and collect donations from others. So, I could say I had some experience in fundraising.

But this was different. When I was living and working in the community, I was not fundraising as a professional. When I asked for donations to the Telshe Yeshiva, for example, I was expected to donate in like manner when the donor asked me for a donation for his charitable cause. So, the experience I had was not so much as fundraising, but trading favors—"you scratch my back, and I'll scratch yours". The difference now would be that I would be asking for money and not giving anything in return. That's a lot harder to do. In the first case I'm cajoling an equal—in the second, I'm begging from a rich man. There was another difficulty. Before, I was raising money for a local institution that the donor or his family or his neighbor was benefiting from, now I would be raising money for a *yeshiva* half a world away.

I hesitated to accept the proposal because I had come to the *Yeshiva* to learn, not to work. But, on the other hand, I wasn't paying tuition (we don't charge tuition to married students) and was benefitting from the wonderful teaching there, so I felt I owed it to *the Rosh HaYeshiva* to help him. It would also afford me a chance to visit my family in the States and to see my friends and former partners. My wife reluctantly agreed, although she wasn't happy with my decision. We had three small children at home at the time, and they would miss their father. I had never been separated from her or them for more than a day or two. My initial trip would be for three weeks—a considerably long period of separation for us. But I like challenges and thought the family could manage without me for a few weeks.

Of course, becoming a schnorrer—Yiddish for the job I was to take on, was not an easy decision to make. I would go from being a respectable member of a learned profession, to a beggar. "Fundraiser" in English has a connotation of a professional in a tuxedo who organizes sumptuous charity dinners at fancy country clubs and hotels where he hobnobs with his guests, the hoi polloi, gives them handsome plaques and gets their donations to his worthy cause. The onomatopoeic Yiddish word *schnorrer* conjures up the image of an oily, dirty and sniveling supplicant, rubbing his hands together when contemplating a handout. If he showed up at the fundraiser's event at the Ritz Carlton, he'd get an unceremonious "heave-ho". Not a very appealing picture. I told myself that I would be different. I would maintain my dignity while serving a very worthy cause. But the image of a *schnorrer* would always haunt me.

Mr. Feinberg

My first trip was in May of 1987. It went very well, particularly for a first trip. I collected a substantial amount of money.

I got my share of refusals, but very few from my friends. My goodwill was still somewhat intact. When I was refused, I felt like the door-to-door Fuller Brush man without the brushes. Not a very comfortable feeling, but I wasn't discouraged—a bit depressed, but not discouraged.

One major success was a visit I made to a non-religious man I had never previously met. As I walked into the office building for an appointment with my friend Brian, I noticed on the marquee that Mr. Feinberg's company headquarters was on the fifth floor. My meeting with Brian ended at 5:00 pm. I had no other appointments until after dinner. I thought to myself, "why not try Mr. Feinberg? You never know what might happen?" I was about to learn a very important lesson.

I stopped off at the fifth floor and entered the reception area. I said to the receptionist, "I'd like to speak to Mr. Feinberg."

"Do you have an appointment?"

"No. But tell him I'm a friend of Irving Stone and happened to be in the building so I thought I'd drop in. I have something I'd like to talk to Mr. Feinberg about."

"What is it?" she asked.

The summer after graduating from college I worked, very briefly, as a dictionary salesman in office buildings in Manhattan. I would go from building to building and office to office lugging this fifteen-pound monster around with me for eight hours or more a day. The dictionary was a photo offset reproduction of the 1904 edition of the Merriam-Webster dictionary with a white leatherette gold-embossed cover. Its copyright had expired, so the only cost to the company was the printing, the paper, and the cover. Our cost was about $3.50 and we sold it for $52.00. Not a bad profit! As salesmen we would get a 25% commission for each one sold. We never actually told our customers that we were selling the dictionary. At first the company had tried selling it, but it seemed that very few people really wanted to buy a dictionary. Then they hit on the idea of giving the dictionary as a gift if the customer would take three – three-year subscriptions from a list of magazines. These were not the top tier of magazines, like *Life, Time,* or *Newsweek,* but maybe second or third tier—like *Hot Rod, 16, Jet,* or *Hairdo*. This proved to be a much better strategy. People love getting something for nothing. Magazines and the print media, in general, don't rely on subscription money to make a profit, but on advertising dollars. The larger the circulation, the more money you can get for your ad space. At no cost to us, these magazines were willing to let our company register subscribers to increase their circulation. We told the customer that he was paying for the magazine subscription, whereas, in reality, he was buying the dictionary. I know, it sounds unsavory. But that's business. It was fun at first, but the fun only lasted for the first week. After that I found it increasingly difficult to lie for profit. I quit after three weeks. But I did learn some useful lessons that helped me in fundraising. Number one was, unless you have an appointment, never tell the secretary or receptionist the real reason you are there. We were also taught to say that we needed to speak with the office manager. If asked why, the answer was: "it's personal." Why the office manager? Because if you could sell a dictionary to the office manager, he or she would help you sell to the other people in the office. It's the nature of people to want others to share their "good fortune" especially if they had to pay for it.

Because there was no territory assigned to each salesman, it often happened that another salesman from our office had been there the week or the day before.

If a receptionist asked me if I was selling dictionaries, my answer would be "no."

"Oh, really?" some asked. "Then what's that in the case you're carrying?"

"Um," I'd say. "It's a dictionary, but I'm not selling it."

"Then what are you selling?"

"I can't talk about it. I need to talk to the office manager, it's personal."

Surprisingly very few would ask me if I knew the name of the office manager, which would be a dead giveaway that it couldn't have been very personal. I would get to speak to one out of three managers. I rarely sold a dictionary.

So now in Mr. Feinberg's office I had several advantages. I at least knew his name (which was on the door) and I knew a friend of his (at least I assumed he was a friend)—wealthy Jews in a small city like Cleveland tend to know each other.

"Do you have a card?" the receptionist asked.

"Yes. Here it is." The card described me as the General

Counsel of Ohr HaTzadikim International, Inc. It seemed a better title than "*Schnorrer.*"

She disappeared and came back a few minutes later.

"Mr. Feinberg will see you now," she said.

I couldn't believe my good fortune. In fact, as I was later to learn, this was beginner's luck. In my career as a fundraiser for the last thirty-four years I never got to meet another billionaire without a hard-won appointment (unless, by chance, I bumped into him, which happened a couple of times).

She showed me into a very large office. Mr. Feinberg asked me to sit down. I had a brochure about the *Yeshiva* and some other pamphlets showing pictures of the campus, the students, and the budget. As I opened my mouth to speak, Mr. Feinberg said:

"Rabbi," (I wasn't one at the time, and my card only identified me as a lawyer) he said, "let me stop you right there."

"How do you spell the name of your organization?"

I told him. He wrote it down.

"Look at the wall behind you."

I turned to look. It was covered with photographs.

"All those photos are of me with every Prime Minister, Foreign Minister and Defense Minister of Israel from Ben Gurion until today."

"Very impressive." I spoke.

"Do you know how many times I've been to Israel?"

"No, I don't."

"Never!" he said. "They all come to me."

I had no idea where this conversation was going.

"Let me tell you about my institution," as I opened the color brochure with the pictures of the *Yeshiva.*

"I'm not interested in hearing about it," he said. "Don't say another word. I'll give you $5000 dollars and not a penny more. But if you start talking, I'll reduce it."

I was shocked. That was an incredibly generous contribution from someone I had never met before. I guess my mouth was hanging open.

"I see you're surprised. I usually get that reaction. Thanks for coming and my secretary will write out a check. Please wait in the reception area. "

I thanked him briefly, not believing my incredible luck. As I sat waiting for the check, I realized that what had happened was total *siyata d'Shmaya*—help from Heaven. My efforts had almost nothing to do with the gift. All I did was show up at his office.

About a year later I was in Cleveland for my second fundraising trip. I had read in the Wall Street Journal that Mr. Feinberg had sold his privately held company to a competitor for close to a billion dollars. I hoped that he might add another zero to the donation of the previous year. His office had moved. He was now in a fancier downtown building. On the marquee in the lobby of the new building it listed his office number as 601. I went to the sixth floor and looked for the number. There was a 599 and 603, but no 601. There was an unlabeled, nondescript door where 601 should have been, but it looked more like a storage closet than an office entrance door. I went down to the lobby and asked the concierge where Mr. Feinberg's office was.

"Mr. Feinberg? I don't know a Mr. Feinberg."

"But I know his office is here and his company is even listed on the marquee as office 601," I said.

"Well, if it's listed, why are you asking me?"

"Because I went up to the sixth floor and couldn't find a door with the number 601."

"Well," he said, "if you can't find it, why do you think I can?"

"Because you're the concierge and you can call them."

"Sorry, I don't have a phone number for them."

Undeterred, I went up to the sixth floor and knocked on the door that should have been 601. No one answered. I knocked harder. No one answered. I sat in front of the door. I had a newspaper and figured I'd stay there for an hour and see if anyone came in. Maybe they were all out to lunch. After about half an hour, the door opened from the inside. A giant of a man in a suit stood in the doorway.

"What do you want?" he asked gruffly.

"I'd like to see Mr. Feinberg."

"Do you have an appointment?"

"No, but I know him. Here's my card."

He closed the door and came back after a few minutes.

"Mr. Feinberg will see you now."

On the other side of the storage closet door, I was greeted by a scene out of a weird dream or movie. The corridor was divided into blocks representing different properties on a Monopoly board. Park Place was lit up by blue neon lights from floor to ceiling. New York Ave. was orange. Atlantic Ave.— yellow. I guess this was a message that Mr. Feinberg had played the real-life game of Monopoly and won. I was ushered into an enormous office and there was Mr. Feinberg behind an impossibly gigantic desk. Behind him was a glass enclosed private elevator. He did not have to use the front door where 601 should have been.

"This is a very impressive office," I said.

"Thanks."

"Could you tell me the meaning of the Monopoly game and

why you don't have a number or name on your door?"

"No."

There was no point in continuing my line of questions.

"I don't know if you remember me, but I visited you in your office last year when it was on Ninth Street."

"I remember," he said. "I'll give you $1000 dollars and not a penny more."

"But" I said, "last year you gave me $5000."

"Yes," he responded. And now I'm giving you $1000."

"Goodbye," he said. "Nice to see you."

The following year I read that Mr. Feinberg had died. I had tried connecting to his son and heir and was able to get his unlisted telephone number. But he wasn't interested in meeting me, and unlike his father he had no office I could camp in front of.

Sr. Calderon

In the late 1990s, a friend of mine from Miami Beach called me. Allan is an ophthalmologist and, as is true for many doctors in Miami, has a large clientele from South America. One of his patients was Sr. Calderon, a very wealthy Jew from Chile. Sr. Calderon had a daughter, Mimi, who had recently become observant. The rest of her family, while traditional, were not *frum*. Her father was very concerned about her going "off the deep end" with her "fanatical" (in his eyes) practice of Judaism, especially since she had decided to come to Jerusalem for a few months of intensive study. In short, she had become a *baalat teshuvah*. Mimi was divorced a couple of times and had three children by her two previous husbands. Her father had confided to Allan, who was also a religious Jew, but not *charedie*, that he was worried about his daughter and wondered if he knew someone in Jerusalem whom she might relate to and might be a modifying influence. Allan thought of my wife and me. We knew each other from Cleveland where Alan did his medical residency at the Cleveland Clinic. My wife is Spanish, and I am also fluent in that language. Alan recommended us and told Sr. Calderon that he would call me with Mimi's contact information and notify me when she arrived in Israel.

Allan called and told me that if we were successful in moderating Mimi's behavior, Sr. Calderon might be so grateful that he might give a large donation to the *Yeshiva*. The mechanics of how I would meet Sr. Calderon were not yet clear, but I figured I'd leave that up to *Hashem*.

When she came to Israel a few months later, we invited Mimi to our home and she and my wife became very fast and close friends. We hosted her on many *Shabbatot* and had dinner with her at her hotel on numerous occasions. She invited us to tour Jordan with her. We accepted. Our accommodations were at the best hotels in Jordan. We visited Petra and ascended *Har HaHor*, the mountain on which *Aaron HaCohen*, *Moshe Rabbeinu's* brother, died and was buried, on the first day of the month of *Av*, his *Yahrzeit*.

Even without the motivation of a potential gift from her father, our friendship with Mimi was sincere. But I would be lying if I didn't have that possible donation in the back of my mind.

While getting to know Mimi we discovered that another very close friend of mine, who had made *Aliyah* a couple of years before us, and who worked as a lawyer for an Israeli defense contractor, had met and become friendly with Mimi's father, who was an arms dealer with significant connections to the Chilean Armed Forces. Sr. Calderon wasn't just rich, he was very, very rich. He also owned the exclusive rights to import all the Japanese and Korean cars to Chile and numerous other businesses. The amount I was going to ask him for as a donation kept doubling by the week.

Finally, my chance came. The following year, with Mimi now back in Santiago, we got a call and an invitation to her son's wedding. Mimi was going to pay all our expenses to come to the wedding and asked that my son Binyamin, then fifteen, whom she had grown fond of, should also accompany us.

This was going to be the wedding of the century in the Chilean Jewish community. Mimi's family was the wealthiest Jewish family in the country and her son was marrying the daughter of the Conservative Chief Rabbi of Argentina.

We arrived two weeks before the wedding and were chauffeured from the airport to our hotel, near the gated community where Mimi and her family lived. She hired a guide for us, and we toured the country from Santiago in the center southward to the Pacific port of Valparaiso, where her family originally settled after coming from Turkey, in the early 1900's.

We met her parents on several occasions before the wedding. I mentioned the names of my friends, the ophthalmologist, and the lawyer, to Mimi's father. I made sure he understood that it was my wife and I who had kept Mimi tethered. I tried to make an appointment with him to discuss the *Yeshiva*. He was very busy, he said, but would try to make time, but it really wasn't a good time to ask for a donation. The wedding must have cost him upwards of half a million dollars, so his argument to me that this was an inopportune time to ask for a donation didn't sound like a cop out. By the time we were to leave Chile, he apologized for not meeting and invited us to come back again in January, summertime in the Southern Hemisphere, and visit him in his summer house in the South and maybe we could talk then. He was a Reserve Rear Admiral in the Chilean Navy and invited me to join him on a Naval cruise to the edge of Antarctica. It sounded very exciting, but not too realistic, since I would need kosher food and would have many issues involving *Shabbos* and other religious obligations.

While we had a very enjoyable time in Chile, it was a bust in terms of fundraising, or so I thought. Every morning my son and I traveled by bus for half an hour to the nearest *shul*. I *davened* with the Kollel, which at the time had about six members. A few other men came to complete the *minyan*. I sat next to an old man in a rumpled flannel shirt. He struck up a conversation with me after *davening* on the first day I came. When he heard that I was from Jerusalem he immediately switched from Spanish to Hebrew. Mr. Friedman was a Holocaust survivor who had come to Israel after leaving a Displaced Persons camp in Germany in 1947. He fought in the Israeli War of Liberation in 1948. Because of his inability to earn a living in Israel he moved to Santiago in the fifties. He did not appear to have improved his lot by the move.

On our last day in Chile, I said goodbye to Mr. Friedman. He asked me to write down the name and address of my *yeshiva* in Jerusalem. I did so on the only business card I had occasion to use in the last two and a half weeks. I thought he wanted to correspond with me. I never asked him for a donation to the *Yeshiva* and if he gave one, I expected, at most, ten dollars, which would represent a generous donation according to my estimation of Mr. Friedman's wealth.

A month later, after I was back in Jerusalem, I got a letter from a lawyer in Tel Aviv, who identified Mr. Friedman as his client. He wanted our banking details so that he could transfer $10,000 to us. Talk about *siyata d'Shmaya*! The person I had hoped to get a donation from gave me nothing and the person that I never solicited gave a substantial sum.

It reminded me of a story I heard from Rav Shraga Weinstein, *z"l,* Founder and *Rosh HaYeshiva* of Ohr HaTzadikim. It took place in London in 1940, shortly after World War II had begun. The city was devastated by Nazi bombing and the people were afraid for their lives. There was a small *yeshiva* in East London by the name of *Toras Emes.* The *yeshiva* had very little money and was in danger of closing. Rav Moshe Schneider, the *Rosh Yeshiva*, gave each *bochur* three addresses. He told them to go to those homes and ask for a donation to the *yeshiva.* A very shy ten-year-old Moishe Sternbach was given his three addresses. He didn't really want to go, but the *Rosh Yeshiva* had spoken. As he approached the first address, he heard the barking of a dog from within. Moishe was deathly afraid of dogs. He ran away and went to the second address. With great trepidation he knocked on the door. "Who's there?" yelled a loud voice. Moishe squeaked out his name, which would have been almost inaudible had the door been open. The man of the house appeared and harshly asked: "What do you want?" Little Moishe, trembling, answered that he was collecting funds for the *Toras Emes Yeshiva.* The man slammed the door in his face.

Shaken, but determined to complete his mission, Moishe took out the paper with the addresses and went to the third. It was a large and imposing mansion surrounded by a high iron fence. As he approached the iron gate, he noticed the sign,

"Beware of Dog". With his tail between his legs, so to speak, Moishe ran back to the *yeshiva* and after learning for a couple of hours, went to bed. In the morning after *shacharis,* the Rosh Yeshiva came over to him, shook his hand warmly and said in a loud voice *"yasher koach (*congratulations*) Reb Moshe"* you saved the *yeshiva.*"

For a moment, Moishe was speechless. Then he said: "I'm sorry, *Rosh Yeshiva,* I think you're making a mistake."

"Did you go to the three addresses I gave you?"

"Yes, but at the first house I heard a dog barking, and I ran away, at the second the owner slammed the door in my face and the third I left after seeing a sign on the fence "Beware of Dog". So, I didn't do anything."

The *Rosh Yeshiva* smiled. "Did you think I expected you to come back with the money we needed to keep the *yeshiva* open? I asked you to do *hishtadlus*—to try. When we make the necessary effort *Hashem* does the rest. This morning before *davening* a wealthy man came to my house and handed me a check for enough to sustain the *yeshiva* for another month. Without your *hishtadlus, Hashem* wouldn't have made it happen."

I love that story and I know it's true. Its message serves as an antidote to the all-too-common feeling that I'm failing as a fundraiser when I get turned down. It's my efforts that support the *Yeshiva*, not the money I collect. Whether I collect the money or someone else does, is irrelevant, I just must try. After more than thirty years of fundraising, I've seen this truth play out time and time again. Sometimes the effort is minimal, and the result is enormous.

Miss Stein

In the early years of my career as a fundraiser, I started to expand my territory. No one from the *Yeshiva* had been to Pittsburgh for many years. My father, *a"h,* was born and raised in a small town near Pittsburgh. I had fond memories of visiting my grandparents there every other *Rosh Hashana,* when I was young. In those years, my grandparents still lived in the tiny three-bedroom house where my father and his five siblings were raised. Behind the house was a large barn, filled with old farm equipment and a few acres of land that my grandfather farmed. He grew vegetables—carrots, peppers, and tomatoes. So, I felt an affinity to the area. There were very few wealthy religious people in Pittsburgh. In fact, it was a poor city in the late 80's and early 90's, when I visited. But it was relatively close to Cleveland, so I thought it might be worth a trip. Like Cleveland, it was in the Rust Belt and the heavy industries that had made both cities great industrial centers in the early part of the 1900's were dead or dying. The difference was that Cleveland was still home to many of the Fortune Five Hundred companies in the States, Pittsburgh was not. I tried my best there but collected very little money and after three trips over three years, I decided not to return.

One of the people I visited was a middle-aged spinster, Miss Stein, who had known the *Rosh HaYeshiva,* Rabbi Weinstein, *z" l,* himself a Pittsburgher, and whose father had been a *Rov* in that city. She was very nice and gave me a check for $52.00 It was one of the largest checks that I collected in Pittsburgh on that trip. About twenty years later, the *Yeshiva* received a letter from a lawyer in Pittsburgh informing us that Miss Stein had died and left us over $100,000 in her will. The only money we ever got from her before was that one donation twenty years earlier. A plaque honoring her generosity now graces a wall in our offices in Jerusalem—another example of *siyata d'Shmaya*.

The Doctor's Will

This past year, I saw another amazing example of a little effort resulting in a large gift. I had met Mordechai, a retired American businessman, at an event that the *Yeshiva* hosted for a mentoring program that matches up American and Canadian college students, at the *Yeshiva* for a two-week program, with visiting religious American and Canadian professionals and businessmen. A few weeks after the program ended, Mordechai called me to ask if I could be in touch with a lawyer in Massachusetts. His uncle, an unmarried Holocaust survivor and physician had recently died in Boston leaving a considerable estate to members of his extended family and to charity. Mordechai had been so impressed with the work we were doing that he wanted to direct some of that charity money to us. Together with the lawyer for the estate, who was also a religious Jew, I was able to craft a memorial to Mordechai's uncle that satisfied the non-religious heirs and the Attorney General's office in Massachusetts, which has oversight of all testamentary gifts to charitable organizations. We were able to secure a six-figure gift to the *Yeshiva*.

Of course, with everything we do, big or small, Heaven is always aiding us. But it's nice to see it in bold relief from time to time.

However, not all my experiences in fundraising have been

positive. I learnt an important lesson when I visited Central America for the *Yeshiva*.

Raul

For many years, my wife taught private classes in Jewish law and philosophy to Spanish-speaking women who wanted to undergo conversion to Judaism in Israel. One of those women was Maria, a young lady from Panama. She seemed very sincere in her desire to convert, and she was also very committed to learning about Judaism. The examination given by the *Beis Din* performing the conversion is comprehensive. The candidate must be prepared to answer questions on *Berachot (blessings), Shabbos, Yom Tov, Kashruth,* details pertaining to menstrual cycles, the life cycle of a Jew, Jewish philosophy etc., etc. Maria was quite bright and picked up the information quickly. After ten months of classes and practice exams, my wife felt she was ready for the conversion *Beis Din*. At that point, Maria introduced us to her boyfriend, a Syrian Jew from Panama who came to our house to thank my wife. My wife knew that Maria had a boyfriend but knew almost nothing about him. Raul was a successful businessman in Panama, and he offered to pay my wife for the classes. My wife refused. She never took payment for these classes. He was very touched, and we became friendly. In speaking to me he found out that among other things, I did fundraising for Ohr HaTzadikim. He had heard of our *Yeshiva* and invited me to come to Panama for a fundraising trip. He told me that he would introduce me to other businessmen who were his friends. I was intrigued. I had never been to Panama and looked forward to visiting a new venue and testing the waters. About six months after they returned to Panama, I was on a plane from New York to Panama City. Raul's driver picked me up at the airport and took me to meet my host at a hotel in the center of town, where I was to stay. It was a few blocks away from a large Syrian *shul* where Raul *davened shacharit*. Afterwards, we went out to dinner with his family at an excellent kosher fish restaurant. When dropping me off at the hotel, he warned me not to venture out after dark, as there were a lot of muggings in the city. The next morning, I went to *shul,* which was guarded by military police with machine guns. There was a guardhouse at the entrance, and I was not permitted to enter the premises without the sponsorship of someone in the community and clearance from the Israeli Embassy. I had my Israeli passport with me and, fortunately, someone was in the embassy office at 7.00 a.m. who confirmed that I was an Israeli citizen. Shortly thereafter, Raul drove up and vouched for me and we went to the *Beit Knesset* to *daven*. The *shul* was beautiful, the *chazzan* had an excellent voice, and the pace was slow. Afterwards, we went for breakfast at one of the many kosher restaurants in town.

We flew to Raul's workplace in the Canal Zone, in his private prop plane. It was raining. Raul told me that it rains a lot in the winter. I was confused. I knew that Panama was a few degrees above the Equator and May is not a winter month in the Northern Hemisphere. I asked him why he said it was "winter"? He explained that the temperature in his country is hot all year round, but from May to November it's very rainy, so they called it "winter" to distinguish it from the "summer" which was relatively dry. The flight was about twenty minutes long. A driver picked us from the airport and drove us to his showrooms—a large four-story building with displays of the clothing brands he represented and that he exported to Central and South America. The Canal Zone is tax and tariff free, so it's the hub of the import-export business in Central America. The businesses there are primarily owned either by Syrian Jews or "Syrian/Palestinian Arabs" who have been in Panama since the early part of the 20th Century. The *lingua franca* is Arabic. All the Jews speak it fluently and all business is conducted in that language. I thought that my Spanish might be an asset to me in Panama, but the truth is that everyone I dealt with spoke English and Hebrew as well as Spanish and Arabic.

The retailers that Raul sold to in Central and South America were almost all Arabs and he spent the day on the phone haggling with them in Arabic.

I spent five days in Panama. Each morning Raul took me to breakfast at a different dairy restaurant and then to dinner at a different meat restaurant. The food was delicious, and Raul was excellent company.

Raul gave me the names of his friends, who were other businessmen in the Canal Zone, and ordered his driver to take me to each address. He called many of his friends prior to my arrival to smooth my entry.

I had very little success in Panama except for Raul. His friends were all Syrian Jews and the idea of giving a substantial donation to an Ashkenazi/Litvish *baal teshuva yeshiva* seemed quite foreign to them. I came away with small donations of $36 and $54 dollars (multiples of 18 which in *gematria*—Jewish numerology—is the numerical value of "life"), no doubt doubled from what I might have otherwise gotten but for Raul's phone call. I was not alone. Everywhere I went I was accompanied by swarms of other *schnorrers,* mostly *Sephardim*, but some *Chassidim* who preceded or followed me to the waiting rooms of the businessmen. I wondered when they had time to conduct their business since the *schnorring* never ceased.

One of the last businessmen I called upon was Raul's brother. His business seemed to be as sizable as Raul's.

I assumed I could get a large donation from him. I was quite surprised when his reaction to me was less than welcoming.

"I understand that your wife was the one who prepared Maria for conversion?"

"That's correct," I answered.

"Are you an Orthodox rabbi?"

"Yes."

"Tell me," he said, "can an Orthodox rabbi officiate at a wedding between a *Cohen* and a *geores*?"

My stomach started turning.

"Of course, not," I answered.

"So how did an Orthodox rabbi marry my brother to a *geores*?"

This was the first time I learnt that Raul was a *Cohen*. My wife told me that she asked his girlfriend if he was a *Cohen* and explained to Maria that a convert was not permitted to marry a *Cohen*. Maria told her that Raul wasn't a *Cohen*.

"I had no idea that you are *Cohanim*," I spoke. Their family name was an Arabic one, so it wasn't a giveaway that they might be *Cohanim*.

"Well," he said, "we are."

"How could an Orthodox rabbi perform the marriage ceremony?" he asked again.

"I don't know, maybe he didn't know your brother is a *Cohen*."

"He did."

I tried to turn the conversation to something less fraught and started to talk about the *Yeshiva*. He wasn't very interested. I got a small donation.

I didn't mention my conversation with his brother to Raul.

Raul gave me a $10,000 check. The trip was financially worthwhile, but it taught me an important lesson.

Upon reflection I realized that Raul wanted to show me off at the kosher restaurants, the kosher supermarkets, and I even joined him for a large Jewish National Fund annual dinner at the Jewish Club. He wanted people to see that I, an Orthodox rabbi with a beard and black hat, endorsed him and his marriage, even though as a Cohen he was prohibited from marrying a convert.

That was the last trip I would make to Panama. And I was sure that if I went again, I wouldn't get as much money, even from Raul. I had served my purpose. And I learned my lesson. Being a religious Jew carries with it a responsibility to investigate every potential situation in which you may be placed. And if you are a rabbi, you have even greater visibility. Just by appearing with a certain person in public you may be giving a stamp of approval to his actions. Be aware that people might be willing to use you for their own unkosher purposes. Your behavior should also be above scrutiny because you are an ambassador for the religious world, the Jewish People and for *Hashem*.

CHAPTER XXIII
My Main Occupation

I'd like to say that my main occupation is learning Torah. But that would be misleading. While I am occupied with learning for part of the day, my main occupation is being the *Menahal* (Director) and General Counsel of Ohr HaTzadikim.

After learning in the *Yeshiva* for about five years, I started teaching. I taught *Gemara* for a short time, which I loved. I had the chance of imparting the tools and methods that I had learned from my teachers to those just beginning.

One day, Reb Shraga, *z'l*, after speaking with Rav Nissan Holderman, *z'l*, asked me if I would be interested in giving a *Chumash* shiur to the *Beis Medrash*. I jumped at the chance. At the time, Reb Nissan, one of the original staff members and the *mashgiach ruchani* (the spiritual leader) of the *Yeshiva* was giving that *shiur* three days a week, I was to give that *shiur* on the other two days.

A year or so after I decided to become *frum,* I had developed a passionate interest in studying the *Chumash* with *Rashi*'s commentary. In fact, the *Chumash* is literally a "closed book" without *Rashi*'s commentary. And not only that, but not learning *Rashi* can cost you money! As it did me.

When I first became religious, at the start of law school, I read the *Chumash* **without** *Rashi*. When I got to *Chumash Vayikra*—the Book of Leviticus, I read that certain animals were clean, and others were unclean. If you touched an unclean one, you had to go through a complicated process to become clean again. It wasn't clear to me whether the uncleanliness was transmitted by dead animals or live ones; whether it applied to just non-kosher animals or kosher ones as well; and what, exactly, this uncleanliness did to a person. Had I read *Rashi* I would have learned that the uncleanliness I was afraid of isn't applicable today; that even in the days of the Temple, it applied mostly to *Cohanim;* and that the *Chumash* was only referring to animals that died of injuries, natural causes or were not slaughtered properly; and myriad other laws that pertain to *tumah and tahara* (the laws of impurity and purity). I was at the stage in my religious development that I didn't think to ask a rabbi about my questions. The reason being that I didn't know enough to know that I had questions.

One of those laws that I didn't know about was that if the skin of the animal, even an unclean one, had been worked into leather it couldn't transmit *tumah* even in Temple times.

I had been an English instructor in a graduate school in Spain before I went to law school and one of my appreciative students bought me a very expensive and beautiful pigskin briefcase (after he received his grade on the final exam and the course).

The day after reading this passage in the *Chumash* I asked a close friend in law school, a non-Jew, to come to my apartment because I had a present for him. Later that day when he came, I took him to the bedroom and pointed to the briefcase (I didn't want to touch it).

"This is for you Bob," I said.

"Thank you very much, but why are you giving this to me?"

"Because I read in the Bible yesterday that I can't touch

pigskin."

He was pleased if not somewhat bewildered by my strange religion.

"That means you can't play football?" he asked.

I also had thought of that.

"Not unless I know that the ball is made of rubber," I answered.

So, as I said, not learning *Rashi* can be expensive.

Rav Holderman told me to make sure that all the week's Torah portion was covered together with the most important *Rashis*. *Rashi* is a succinct commentary by Rabbi Shlomo Yitzchaki (whose initials spell out "*Rashi*" in Hebrew). *Rashi* (1040-1105) was born and lived most of his life in Troyes, in Northern France. In those days, being a rabbi was not a paying job. To make a living *Rashi* was a wine merchant. In fact, almost all the great rabbis of the Middle Ages were also engaged in businesses or professions. In Spain, the main profession for rabbis seems to have been medical doctor. Some of our greatest rabbis from that time, like *Rambam* (Maimonidies) and *Ramban* (Nachmanides) were physicians, as were many others. My wife, who is a descendant of the *Ramban*, also has many doctors in her family tree.

According to *Rashi's* own statements, the purpose of his commentary on the *Chumash* was to explain *pshat*—the plain meaning of the text. In the rare instances where he deviates, it's because the plain meaning of the words gives a misleading understanding of what is being said.

While many commentaries will explain a *posuk* (verse) with tens or hundreds of words, *Rashi* will suffice with a sentence or two. And his sentences are not enigmatic, but perfectly clear. It is for this reason that his commentary on the

Chumash is the most reprinted. His commentary on the *Gemara* is likewise known for his economy of words and clarity of explanation and is also the most widely reprinted and quoted commentary on the Talmud. It never ceases to amaze me how one person could have achieved what *Rashi* achieved during a lifetime. And all that while running a successful wine business. In fact, I'm in awe of contemporaries like Rabbi Pinchas Kehati, *z'l*, who wrote a massive and widely used commentary on all the *mishnayos*, part of it while working as a bank clerk in Jerusalem. I have no idea how anyone could accomplish such a daunting task.

I have felt a spiritual kinship with *Rashi* (all Jews are ultimately related to each other, since we are all descended from common ancestors). We do share the same Hebrew first name, Shlomo, and after having named our first two daughters Miriam and Rochel (without any conscious thought to *Rashi*), when our third daughter was born, my wife suggested that her name should be Yocheved—just like *Rashi*'s three daughters—Yocheved, Miriam and Rochel. *Rashi*'s daughters married his students. They and their progeny wrote the famous commentary on the *Gemara* and on *Rashi*'s commentary, known to all scholars as *Tosofos*—certainly among the greatest rabbis in our history.

After giving that *shiur* in *Chumash* for a couple of years, I grew tired of the perfunctory nature of my lectures. I wanted to explore the *Rashis* in much more detail. I wanted to know why *Rashi* commented on those passages he did, and why he didn't on others. Also, there are several places where *Rashi* comments; "I don't know what this means." Imagine that—a scholar who admits, in writing, to not understanding something rather than just skipping over it! A book by Rabbi Dr. Avigdor Boncek,

"What was Bothering *Rashi*?" later popularized this method of examination. This approach to *Rashi* was almost 1000 years old. Many rabbis had written extensively on these questions. The commentary I focused on is called the *Gur Aryeh*. It was written by the *Maharal M'Prague*, Rabbi Yehuda Lowy, universally famous for the story of the *Golem*—a humanoid that Rabbi Lowy had *Kabbalstically* created and who served as a protector of the sixteenth century Jewish community of Prague. We don't know if the stories of the *Golem* are true. They probably aren't. The *Maharal* left no written mention of the *Golem*. And it does seem to beggar belief. But, as his genius and mastery of Torah and *Kabbalah* is clear from his writings, if he wanted to create a *Golem*, he probably could have. The *Gur Aryeh* is his deep examination of *Rashi*'s commentary.

As an example, let's look at a *posuk* in the Torah. In *Parshas Yisro* (Exodus 18:1 – 20:23), *Yisro* (Jethro), the father-in-law of Moshe, after hearing about the parting of the Red Sea and the Israelites war with Amalek, travels from his home in Midian to the Israelites' encampment in the desert with Tzipora, Moshe's wife and their two sons, Gershom and Eliezer.

To recount, Moshe, while still living as a prince in Pharaoh's palace, but retaining his sense of Jewish identity, sees an Egyptian guard beating an Israelite, and kills him. Hunted by the Egyptian police for the murder, he flees to Midian where he meets some shepherd girls at a well, who are being harassed by a group of male shepherds. These girls, sisters, are the daughters of *Yisro,* a high priest of the Midianite idolatrous religion, who because of his heretical questioning of the basis of their faith, has rendered his family a pariah to its adherents and an object of persecution. Moshe chases away their abusers; helps them to water their flock; and is invited by *Yisro,* to share a meal with the family. After getting to know him and obviously impressed with the nobility (after all, he had been a prince) and chivalry of Moshe, *Yisro* gives his daughter *Tzipora* to Moshe for a wife. Moshe settles down to a life as a shepherd in Midian. After his encounter with G-d at the Burning Bush, G-d tells him to return to Egypt and save his people. Moshe tells his wife about his mission and the family sets out for Egypt. Before they arrive, Aharon, Moshe's brother, meets up with them and tells Moshe to send his wife and children back to his father-in-law, because Egypt is not a place conducive to their well-being. They return, and Moshe and Aharon continue their journey to Egypt. After the Ten Plagues, the Israelites leave Egypt and start on their journey to the Promised Land. Their circuitous route takes them to the banks of the Red Sea where Pharaoh and his army, in hot pursuit of their former slaves, appear and the Israelites seem trapped between the Sea on one side and the Egyptian Army on the other. The Sea miraculously splits, and the Jews make their way through the dry seabed with the Egyptian Army in hot pursuit. After they cross, the split sea converges and the Egyptian Army, now in the middle of the seabed, drowns. Now on the other side of the sea, and safe from their pursuers and with a great fortune garnered from the bejeweled chariots and other valuable objects carried by the Egyptians, which washed up on the shore, the Israelites resume their journey to the Land of Caanan, through the desert, only to be met by the powerful Amalekite army who attacks them. The Jews are miraculously victorious.

At this point, *Yisro* appears at the camp of the Israelites with Moshe's wife and his sons. The Torah relates:

"And he said to Moshe, I, your father-in-law, Yisro have come to you and your wife and her two sons with her." (Shemos

18:6).

This *posuk* might seem simple enough, but it's not. I would ask my students to concentrate on the words of the *posuk* for five minutes without saying anything; to examine the sentence structure; the grammar; the vocabulary; the punctuation; and try to think of any anomalies that *Rashi* should address.

The first thing that we notice is that the words: "*And he said to Moshe,*" can't mean that *Yisro* is speaking directly to Moshe, because, if so, why would Yisro have to explain who he is or who Moshe's wife and children are?

Rashi addresses this questions and comments that when the Torah says "He says to Moshe" the word in Hebrew "*el*" can't be translated as "to" in a direct sense, as it normally is, rather, a communication to an agent, to tell Moshe that Yisro and Moshe's family have come.

The second question is why did Yisro separate himself from Tzipora and the children? A third and related question is: why did he separate the children from Tzipora?

He said, "*I, **Yisro** have come **and** your wife **and** her two sons with her*"—indicating three separate groups. He could have more easily said, "I, Yisro have come with your wife and two children." Why not lump them all together?

Also, we notice that it says that "**her** two sons" have come with her. Aren't they also Moshe's two sons?

Rashi answers these questions by rephrasing Yisro's answer as follows:

"*If you don't want to come out for my sake, come out for the sake of your wife, and if you don't want to come out for the sake of your wife, come out for the sake of her two children.*"

This parsing of the *posuk* makes clear that there are indeed three statements being made by Yisro and they are a hierarchy of "sakes." But the question arises, what are the differences in each group and, in Yisro's mind, why would Moshe treat each group differently?

We can understand from *Rashi* that Yisro is thinking that Moshe might not want to honor him because he was a former idol worshipper. But, even so, he still might want to honor his wife, who had converted to Judaism before marrying Moshe. But, perhaps, he might not want to honor his wife, since she is the daughter of a former idol worshipper and a convert. In any case, surely, he would want to honor his sons by coming out to greet them.

The *Gur Aryeh*, in his commentary on *Rashi*, refers to the *Chizkuni's* question, which shines a light on another question that we have missed. Why did Yisro seek honor from Moshe?

"A question arises here, Yisro, who was such a great man, [why] would he run after honor by saying: "come out for my sake?"

This is not a question. This is not a statement of running after honor, only of avoiding embarrassment. Every person, even a tzadik (saintly person) and a pious [person] feels embarrassment (when not treated with respect). And.... particularly when the guest is Moshe's father-in-law. If Moshe doesn't come out to meet him it would be a great embarrassment and dishonor to Yisro, and Moshe should do so just to save him from embarrassment. This is not running after honor at all..." Gur Aryeh.

In this comment we see a great lesson. I would have thought that together with the idea that we should flee from honor, as we are taught in *Pirkei Avos* (the *Ethics of the Fathers 4:21*), we might also be required to not feel embarrassment when others treat us with disrespect. But that is not so.

And in answer to my questions, the *Gur Aryeh* quotes his brother, Rabbi Chaim from Varnkvort, who cites a *Gemara* in *Sanhedrin* 82a, which discusses an event toward the end of Israelites' journey through the desert. Zimri, a prince of the tribe of Shimon, has relations with a Midianite princess in full view of the Jewish People. Upon being reminded of the law by Pinchas, Moshe orders that they both be killed because that behavior in those circumstances is punishable by death. The members of Zimri's tribe taunt Moshe, seemingly with the same accusation, and say:

"*Who permitted you to marry the daughter of Yisro (an idol worshiper).*"

Therefore, Yisro said: "come out for my sake" that people shouldn't say that you're embarrassed because I'm a non-Jew and I'm not fit to be joined to the Holy Spirit, and this would be an embarrassment to me. And if you don't care about me, at least come out for your wife's sake, that people shouldn't say, 'who permitted her to you?' since she's a non-Jewess and if you don't care about her honor, because you could divorce her, come out for her two sons, because people might say that the child of a non-Jewess is also not Jewish, therefore it says: come out for her two sons, and it doesn't say his two sons." Gur Aryeh.

Meaning—"you, Moshe, should uphold your own honor and the honor of your wife and children first by coming out to greet me, your father-in-law, and then by coming out to greet your wife and children. Because if you don't, people might think you have something to be ashamed of. Maybe your wife didn't properly convert before marrying you and therefore, your children aren't Jewish, they're *her* children, the children of a non-Jew and not yours." This is another level of meaning in

Yisro's words. The following *posuk* shows how Moshe reacted. "And Moshe went out to meet his father-in-law and he bowed down to him and kissed him…" Yisro need not have worried.

If you were bored by the above analysis, you will understand why I didn't attract too many students to my class. But those few who shared my passion, loved it. When I started traveling more often for fundraising, I stopped giving the *shiur* altogether.

CHAPTER XXIV
The Hanhala

In 2006 I was asked to join the *Hanhala* of the *Yeshiva*. The *Hanhala* is the internal Board of Directors. Two members had recently resigned for personal reasons so two slots were open. There were, at the time, five of us, including the two Roshei *Yeshiva* – Reb Shraga, z'l and Reb Noson. It was an offer that I had no reason to expect but felt very honored to receive.

When I first came to the *Yeshiva* as a student, I was in awe of the *rebbeim*. They were so knowledgeable and so articulate. My wildest dream was that one day I too might be qualified to teach in Ohr HaTzadikim. You can imagine my thrill when I was asked to teach. But, after teaching for about ten years, I was suffering from a bit of burnout. While I loved the interaction with students, I was too independent to follow a curriculum. I was also getting much more active in fundraising. I traveled to the United States, Canada, England, France, South and Central America and even to Australia. I started concentrating on a few cities in the States, developing the fundraising there to the point where I felt we needed a full-time fundraiser living in the community, who could teach and raise money. Over the course of the next few years, I would travel to Miami, Cleveland, and Los Angeles about six times a year. And eventually we placed our people in those communities.

I delayed my decision to become a member of the *Hanhala* because it would involve a serious time commitment. I would now become much more involved in the running of the *Yeshiva*. Before, my working time was limited to my teaching, fundraising trips and the occasional legal advice. But now I would have to really make Ohr HaTzadikim my focus. After consulting with my *rebbe,* Rav Moshe, *z'l,* and my wife, I decided to accept.

I mentioned that I am also the General Counsel of the Y*eshiva.* Many people have asked me why a *yeshiva* needs an in-house lawyer? My answer, "You'd be surprised."

Ohr HaTzadikim is a large organization. The *Yeshiva* is a school for young men who, depending on the program, are either post high school or post college. We have approximately 300 full time students, including married students, and about 100 faculty and staff. Our student population increases when our summer and winter programs are in session by approximately another two hundred per year. Ohr HaTzadikim International, Inc., a U.S. based charitable organization, also conducts programming and events in the U.S. and Israel in coordination with similar Canadian and U.K charitable organizations. And while I'm not operationally involved in these foreign organizations, I must be aware of the estate planning, tax, insurance, corporate and non-profit organization laws of the countries in which they are situated, as well as those in Israel. The interaction between the various charitable organizations both foreign and domestic also present many knotty legal problems. In addition, I negotiate contracts with our staff members, as well as satisfy many demands of various governmental bodies on our organization. Labor law in Israel is complicated and issues arise constantly. We've had civil lawsuits and *dinei torah* (disputes in rabbinic courts) with some past employees. In Israel we have been involved with developing a large tract of land that we bought, we lease the land on which our *Yeshiva* is situated and lease another tract nearby. We've had disputes with our development partners and professional advisors. I've had to employ and supervise outside attorneys and rabbinic lawyers for our court related matters here. In short, there's plenty of legal work.

As a member of the *Hanhala*, I try to ensure the smooth running of the *Yeshiva* daily. And it does entail quite a lot of work, but I feel honored to be able to contribute to such a wonderful organization. I'm also involved in our weekly online magazine, which has very interesting articles about the weekly Torah portion, *Gemara*, the Hebrew Language and understanding prayer. I serve as a content editor and occasionally contribute profiles of students and staff members.

CHAPTER XXV
My Politics

Despite my living in Israel, I remain a proud and patriotic American. Recent events in the USA have had their impact on me, as well as on other Americans living here.

Growing up Jewish on Long Island meant that you were a Democrat. In fact, there were only two Jewish kids in my class in high school who identified themselves as Republicans. One was the son of a local Republican judge and the other was unfortunately very mentally unstable and committed suicide in our senior year. My high school had a majority of Jewish students. During the Presidential Campaign prior to the 1964 election, the son of the judge, who, I believe had his own political aspirations, was the lone student willing to take the side of Arizona Senator Barry Goldwater's Republican candidacy in a debate in the school auditorium. For those who don't know or never heard of Senator Barry Goldwater, he was the first major party presidential candidate who had Jewish roots. He himself wasn't Jewish, since he had a Christian mother, but his father was Jewish. It's a little-known fact, but many Jews in the middle to late 1800's, when escaping the anti-Semitism in Eastern Europe, settled in small towns and cities all over the United States hoping to take advantage of their talents for trading and commerce to areas outside of the American "Pale of Jewish Settlement", which was concentrated in the largest cities, like New York, Philadelphia and Chicago.

A few embraced Christianity as a way of getting ahead in small town America. I had a friend in college who, when learning that I was planning to be a lawyer one day, asked me to help him reclaim his great uncle's estate. It seems that this uncle, the young Moishe Horowitz, left his family and *shtetl* in Lithuania and immigrated to the United States in the early 1890's. He went straight to the Arizona Territories (the real "Wild West" with gunslingers and cowboys and Indians) where he thought he could make his fortune in the silver mines. He had no intention of working the mines but being an owner of them. This plan had some difficulties seeing that Moishe had no money and wasn't as strong or as good with a gun as the rough and tumble miners. But he had something that they didn't—a *Litvak* brain. The Catholic Church of Arizona, through generous donations by landowners and royal gifts and grants when the territory belonged to Spain, was a major landowner in the territory. Moishe decided, purely for monetary reasons, to become a Catholic priest. There were few priests in the Territory at the time and Moishe, being a bright and motivated lad, got ordained in record time. He learnt Latin and English and after twenty years became a bishop, the highest-ranking prelate in Arizona. Apparently, he did not take his vow of poverty too seriously and along his path to high office managed to acquire ownership of many productive silver mines. He died in 1921 and left his entire estate, worth millions of dollars, to his family back in the *shtetl*. But his family were *frum yidden* (religious Jews) and when they learnt, years before, that Moishe had become a priest, they sat *shiva* for him, as if he was dead. They wanted nothing to do with his tainted money—no matter how many millions it was.

The Horowitz family eventually left Lithuania and settled

in Brooklyn, and while still identifiably Jewish, were not as intolerant of their apostate uncle as their European forebears had been. They were willing to let bygones be bygones and take the money. Unfortunately for them the Arizona thirty-year statute of limitations for reversing the escheat of an unclaimed decedent's estate had passed. But my friend thought that maybe a smart Jewish lawyer could find his way around that statute. Maybe so, but that lawyer wasn't me.

The point of that story is that although Barry Goldwater had a Jewish father and there was a measure of Jewish pride in his candidacy, there were only two Jews in my high school who supported him. The Democrats portrayed him in one very negative television ad (famously nicknamed "Daisy" because of its depiction of a little girl peacefully picking the leaves of a daisy when a nuclear explosion causes her to vanish from the screen) as a raving lunatic warmonger, who was almost a guarantor of bringing nuclear holocaust to the world. He was no such thing. Although he was a conservative Republican, he was also a supporter of Civil Rights for Negroes (as they were then called) and a war hero who rose to the rank of Major General in the Air Force during WWII.

Jews were Democrats and so was I until I went to Law School. I hadn't really thought deeply about politics or the governmental system before. But now I was learning about the procedural and substantive aspects of the law; the theories behind the law; the working of the judicial system, and how it integrated with the other two branches of government—the legislative and executive. I became conservative, not because my values had changed, but because I came to see government as an inappropriate legislator of moral values and overly intrusive in the lives of its citizens. I understood the need for regulation of many things, like environmental issues, air and water quality, discrimination in housing and the workplace, but I failed to see how it was beneficial to regulate many other things that the government was regulating.

A good example of this was affirmative action in admission standards in higher education, which happened to be a hot topic when I was attending law school. The U.S. Supreme Court heard the case of *DeFunis vs. Odgegaard* 416 U.S. 312 (1974) during my second year of law school. The facts of the case are as follows: the petitioner, Marco DeFunis, Jr., a white Sephardic Jewish student, had been denied admission to the University of Washington Law School. Marco sued in Washington State court and argued that he should have been admitted because his testing scores were higher than many minority students who had been accepted. He claimed that his U.S. Constitutional 14th amendment rights were violated because he suffered discrimination based on his race. After he brought his lawsuit, the University allowed him to enter the following year. By the time the case reached the U.S. Supreme Court it decided that the case was moot, since Marco was graduating from the law school he sued. They declined to decide the issue on its merits.

However, earlier, when the case was argued before the Washington State Supreme Court, the decision went against DeFunis. I liked the dissenting opinions.

Dissenting Justice Hale of that Court said:

"Preferential treatment under the guise of 'affirmative action' is the imposition of one form of racial discrimination in place of another. The questions that must be asked in this regard are: must an individual sacrifice his right to be judged on his own merit by accepting discrimination based solely on the color of his skin? How can we achieve the goal of equal opportunity for all if, in the process, we deny equal opportunity to some?"[3]

Justice Hunter concurred with his colleague Justice Hale:

"The majority supports a laudable purpose—to enable students of certain minority races to enter the University of Washington School of Law in order that ultimately there will be a greater representation of practicing lawyers of those races in the legal profession—with which purpose I do not disagree. This must not be accomplished, however, by clear and willful discrimination against students of other races as the Admissions Committee of the University of Washington School of Law has done in this case by denying admission to the respondent, Marco DeFunis, Jr, to this school, as found by the trial court and amply supported by the record." [3]

This case was debated in the classrooms and the hallways. I was squarely on Marco's side. I suppose an important factor for me was the history of discriminatory policies toward Jews in higher education in America. Before WWII, Jews were commonly excluded from elite universities, like the Ivy Leagues. We were not from the "gentlemanly class" of WASPs. We had no family connections to those schools and were looked down upon as the sons and daughters of peddlers and laborers. This was not just true of Jews, but, of course, blacks and even working-class Catholics. Entry into Law Schools or Medical Schools of the elite Universities was likewise restricted because of race and religion. And this was not only true in the US, but, as I learnt from the famous "resfusenik," Rabbi Dr. Eliyahu Essas, even in the so-called "classless" and non-discriminatory USSR where only a handful of Jews were admitted to the top Universities.

Even when I was in high school, the Ivy Leagues had a

subtle version of the quota system. They couldn't openly exclude Jews, so they based their admissions on geographical representation. Brooklyn, Queens, Nassau County, and parts of Westchester, with a very high percentage of Jewish applicants, were allotted a very small number of slots and an equal number went to South Dakota and Montana. In my high school class, which was approximately 70% Jewish, for example, only the valedictorian, a Protestant, was accepted to Princeton. Harvard hadn't accepted anyone from my school in the previous two years, when it accepted the valedictorian. So, the idea of being excluded from universities because of a quota system was something I had known about since I was young. And now the American government was encouraging a reverse quota system. Blacks were given preferential entry to universities and medical and law schools because of their race and that meant fewer places for those who were more academically qualified. I felt this was grossly unfair.

One of my professors had written about this policy in an article published at the end of my first year in law school. Paul Gershon Haskell's article in the American Bar Association Journal, titled *Legal Education on the Academic Plantation,* 60 A.B.A. J. 203 (1974) caused an uproar in the American legal community. Professor Haskell was my Property Law professor in my first year of law school. He has been compared to Professor Kingsford in the movie *The Paper Chase* (if you haven't seen it, you really should). He was born in Boston, the brilliant son of middle-class Jewish parents. He went to public primary school and Boston Latin (the elite public high school in that city) and received a full scholarship to Harvard. I had heard that he graduated first in his class in Harvard undergraduate school and then first in his class at Harvard Law School. After working for ten years at two of the top "white shoe" New York law firms, he started his teaching career. Although he had an air of intellectual coldness and a stern and exacting classroom manner that scared most of us, he cared very much about his students. As an example, he had scheduled the final exam for the first day of *Shavuos* and when I told him that I couldn't come to school that day because of the holiday, he immediately agreed to let me take it after *yom tov*. I treasured the A- that I earned in that very difficult full year course, which was the second highest grade he gave that year to our class of 120 students.

In his article, based solely on his own observations and conversations with other professors and students, he acknowledged the sins of slavery and racial discrimination, and very logically argued that although he agreed with the goal of encouraging more Blacks to enter the professions, by patronizing those Black students who were not as academically qualified as most of the white students in their law school class, we were harming them irreparably. In his experience many Blacks, because they were ill prepared for the rigors of law school, ended up either flunking out or ending up in the bottom of the class. He imagined what that might do to their feelings of self-esteem.

He was roundly criticized by academics on the left and Black law students. In *A Response to Professor Haskell's Academic Plantation Theory,* A.B.A. Journal, V<u>ol. 60, No. 12 (December 1974),</u> Professor Samuel C. Thompson, Jr.,
himself a beneficiary of preferential admission to an elite law school, argued with the premise of Haskell's article and claimed it to be mostly myth. He said that his experience was positive, and that preferred admission is necessary.

However, as much as Professor Thompson claims that Haskell was wrong, my own observations bear Haskell out. In my class in law school, two of the class's top ten graduates were Black women. They didn't need preferred admission and could've gone to a more elite law school than the one they attended, but, because their husbands both worked in Cleveland, they went to Case Western Reserve. (One of them was the wife of a janitor at a local college and the other was the wife of a prominent attorney at a top law firm in town.)

Those two Black women graduates, although getting jobs with top law firms upon graduation, experienced condescension, at least in their first years of practice, from other lawyers, who didn't know them, thinking that they only had their jobs because of their race. And that's unfair because it wasn't true. But we also had several male Black students who were at the bottom of the class and I'm sure that their self-esteem was damaged.

Professor Haskell's assessment was also borne out in a case before the Ohio Supreme Court in the year I took the Ohio Bar Exam. It involved about thirty Black plaintiffs who had taken the Bar Exam the year before. The overall pass rate on the exam was seventy percent. The plaintiffs claimed that the pass rate for Blacks was around thirty percent. They sued the Bar Examiners for discrimination. Their main obstacle was that the test was anonymous. We were each assigned a number before we took the Bar Exam and only that number identified us on our exam papers. To ensure that there would be no nepotism or discrimination, the test was graded by the examiners with no access to the key identifying the test takers. The results were published by number. These plaintiffs claimed, without any proof whatsoever, that the examiners had gotten hold of the key with the names and numbers and scoured the lists and somehow identified the Blacks (this could only be with their names, since the Bar examiners had no pictures of us) and failed them. The case was dismissed without even a hearing since their complaint didn't allege any evidence of their claim. The case only showed that instead of improving their situation, these Black law school graduates were frustrated in the end, because the Bar Exam was color blind and being Black couldn't help them pass. Imagine their rage at the system, which cost them three years of their life in law school, and then their feelings of failure. In later cases in many other courts and in articles in Law Review journals, the argument was made that the bar exams were either biased against Blacks because they had hidden cultural biases or were unnecessary because they were unpredictable indicators of the ability to practice law. To my knowledge only Wisconsin allows admission to the bar without a bar exam and Black students continue to fail at higher rates than white students in almost every state.

In any case, such arguments about affirmative action also pushed me in the direction of conservatism. In 2022, the U.S. Supreme Court heard arguments in two cases which directly challenged the use of racial and ethnic preferences in university admissions: *Students for Fair Admissions v. Harvard,* 600 U.S. 181 (2023), *and Students for Fair Admissions v. University of North Carolina, No. 21-707.* On 29 June 2023, affirmative action was declared unconstitutional by overwhelming majorities.

Another issue was abortion. Early in my practice as a lawyer, my close friend and colleague, Yanky Weissman and I attended a couple of meetings of the Right to Life movement in Cleveland Heights. We went as unofficial representatives of Cleveland's *frum* community.

Roe vs. Wade U.S. 410 U.S. 113 (1973) had been decided a few years earlier, making abortion legal in all fifty states in the US.

As religious Jews we felt that this was a dangerous development since one reading of Jewish Law holds that a non-Jew who aborts a fetus after the time of conception is guilty of murder, unless the birth or the pregnancy is a threat to the mother's life. A country that allowed women to get abortions without any reason was a country that condoned murder and was in danger of collapse. We wanted to show our solidarity with the Right to Life movement. But aside from us, everyone else at the meeting was Catholic, and although they did everything they could to make us feel comfortable, we weren't. After two meetings we stopped attending. But we were supportive of their efforts to change the law. Republicans eventually made it one of their platform issues. That too pushed me to the right.

There is, of course, a bit of a contradiction here in my belief system. I stated earlier that I believe it's not the government's business to meddle in matters of personal morality. Obviously, there must be exceptions where those matters involve non-consenting victims. For example, there are people who enjoy getting drunk. If the drunk isn't bothering anyone else, I would say: "Let him be." But, if he starts to harass people in the bar, or walks down a city street after leaving the bar and sings at the top of his lungs at 2:00 a.m., waking people up, he should be arrested. Likewise, if he endangers people by driving his car, he should be jailed. But, if he drunkenly walks down the street weaving from side to side or wants to sleep in an alley, "leave him be." He shouldn't be arrested because he offends my moral sensibilities by exhibiting public drunkenness.

However, there are consensual acts between adults, like euthanasia, or dueling, which shouldn't be sanctioned by society nor turned a blind eye to. If two people wish to duel and sign a document absolving each from the murder of the other, should this deter society from legislating against such activity? No? Why not? Because the society has a positive interest in keeping its citizens alive, no matter how little they think of their own lives. A great example of this is the Burr-Hamilton duel. Both men were highly educated, talented and successful. Burr had been the vice president of the United States and Hamilton its first Secretary of the Treasury. They were highly valued members of society. The fact that they hated each other enough to kill, rightly did not absolve Burr for the murder of Hamilton. Society's interest is paramount. Society shouldn't sanction murder. Likewise, even if a group claims that their religion regards stealing as an obligatory act and that through that act their deity is exalted, that should not inhibit a government from passing laws prohibiting theft. In other words, the United States of America was founded under an ethical system that incorporated the Ten Commandments. So, if the society defines abortion as murder of a fetus – a potential life in being, then it is the obligation of society to prohibit it.

The debate between the "right to lifers" and the "pro choicers" is essentially how one sees abortion. The "pro-choice" position is that a woman's body is hers to do with it what she wants and if she wishes to cut off a limb or pierce her nose or cut out her fetus she can do so. The fetus is just like an unwanted appendage. It has no separate existence, no matter what trimester her pregnancy. The other side argues that the fetus is not just another appendage, but a separate life that society needs to protect from harm. We may debate when the fetus becomes more than a mass of cells and tissues and acquires personhood, but that is largely a religious debate and one that has little place in a secular society. If Judaism says it starts from forty days and Catholicism says it begins at conception and Protestants say they're not sure, that's all well and good, but at some point, before birth, when the fetus could survive without its mother, we can all agree that it is a separate life. This doesn't violate the opinion that government has no right to meddle in matters of *personal* morality. A viable fetus is not a matter of personal morality; it's a matter of public morality in the context of the foundational principles assumed in the establishment of the United States.

In its Solomonic decision, the Supreme Court in *Roe* actually "split the fetus". It recognized a woman's Fourteenth Amendment "right to privacy", which allowed her an unrestricted right to choose to abort during the first trimester of her pregnancy, a time it deemed that the fetus wasn't viable. During the second trimester it recognized the government's interest in protecting "prenatal life", as well as women's health and, therefore, laws which balance those rights are constitutional. In the third trimester government could prohibit abortions so long as the law allowed for abortions where the mother's life was in danger. By recognizing both the rights of the mother and the fetus, the Supreme Court struggled through the same moral dilemma that faced us – women's health and choice on one hand and the fetus' right to life on the other. But we viewed their decision as a "slippery slope" to unrestricted abortion and therefore, murder.

Almost fifty years after *Roe* was decided, the United States Supreme Court *in Dobbs vs. Jackson Women's Health*

Organization (June 24, 2022) overruled *Roe* and *Casey* (a 1992 U.S. Supreme Court case), affirming the Constitutional right to abortion). As of today, there is no U.S. Constitutional right for a woman to have an abortion. However, the individual States may decide to allow them or restrict them. The Supreme Court has not recognized a right to life of a fetus, as a "person" protected by the U.S. Constitution, but individual States might. The battleground has now shifted to the State Legislatures.

Another issue I had with the Left was the Welfare system in the US, which was, in my opinion, a disaster. There were programs that I thought necessary to keep people alive, like the Food Stamp Program, Medicare, or Medicaid for those without employment and the ability to pay for medical treatment, and support to families where the breadwinner was disabled. But I also heard of tremendous fraud. Section 8, which subsidized housing for poor people was one that I was very familiar with. I knew of families in which the parents were not civilly married, and while the husband might have a job and earn a respectable wage, his wife reported that she was a single mother with many children and received Food Stamps, WIC (Women, Infants and Children Food aid), Section 8, Medicaid, etc. Other recipients I knew, owned nothing in their name, but received support from their parents and were also recipients of the foregoing benefits. These were not isolated cases, but quite common. Our tax money was going to support people and families who were stealing from the government and the government was doing little to stop it.

Ronald Reagan made welfare fraud a major campaign theme and that appealed to me. I had no problem with government support for those who were incapable of supporting themselves, but not those who were gaming the system.

Republicans, at least, paid lip service to the need to be careful guardians of the public funds. After Reagan's election I don't think anything changed. To really crack down on fraud, you would need aggressive inspectors who took the time to make serious investigations into fraud and there is not enough money allocated to investigators to make a difference. So, the fraud continued even through Republican administrations.

There were other issues that were particularly close to the Orthodox Jewish Community. Jewish Religious Day Schools are very expensive. Today in New York, LA or Miami tuition can average between $15,000 and $40,000 per year, per child. In the rest of the country, it's a bit cheaper, but still very expensive.

Some states have instituted a voucher scheme for parents with children in private schools in certain school districts where the public schools are poorly funded and the district's scores on state exams are under the state average. Those who believe that the First Amendment to the U.S. Constitution prohibits these subsidies to parents who wish to send their children to parochial schools, do so because they are, in effect, State support of religion. These were generally Democrats. I understood their point but didn't see that as a direct support of religion, only an indirect one and therefore Constitutional. The Republicans were on our side of the issue.

And, of course, there was Israel. From 1924 until after WWII, America was quite hostile to all immigration in general and Eastern European and Asian immigration, in particular. Both Republicans and Democrats were complicit. In June of 1939, Roosevelt, on the advice of his Secretary of State, Cordell Hull, even refused a boatload of Jews fleeing Nazi Germany from landing in the United States and sent them back to Europe to their almost certain deaths. Roosevelt did nothing during the war (like bombing the rail lines to the Death Camps) to stop the Nazis from continuing their murder of Jews in the Death Camps even though he knew about it. However, after the end of the Second World War, the Democratic Party became friendlier to the Jews and their dreams of establishing the new State of Israel. Without Democratic Truman's support, the recognition of the State of Israel by the United Nations might not have happened. Jews didn't forget that decision and the Democratic Party cemented its ties with the American Jews.

After Eisenhower, a Republican, was elected in 1952, the hostility of the anti-Semitic State Department to the fledgling State became more evident. In 1956, after Egypt's Gamal Abdel Nasser, an Arab Nationalist, nationalized the Suez Canal, Israel, in cooperation with Great Britain and France, invaded the Sinai Peninsula and wrested the Canal from the Egyptians. They expected the United States to remain neutral, but the Secretary of State, John Foster Dulles and Eisenhower, upset at the British, French and Israelis for not informing them of their plans, sided with Egypt and forced them to return their gains. Jews wouldn't forget how the Republicans had abandoned Israel.

But in 1973, with the Yom Kippur War, the Nixon administration showed itself to be very supportive of Israel. We now had a Jewish Secretary of State, Henry Kissinger, a German born refugee who came to the States as a teenager with his family before WWII and lived in Washington Heights—a religious German-Jewish enclave in Manhattan. (My wife and I even met Henry's parents at a kosher hotel in Mallorca, Spain in the 1970's). It now seemed to me that the Republicans had become kosher as well.

In any case, I felt comfortable in the Republican Party until the election of 2008, when John McCain, whom I thought was a fine choice for President, chose Sarah Palin as his running mate for Vice President. I felt very uneasy. Sarah was a heartbeat away from the Presidency and seemed to me to be a full-fledged ignoramus and nut. It appeared that she had no knowledge of anything outside of moose hunting, moose skinning and moose cooking. And even worse, she seemed to have no interest in learning anything. In my opinion she was unqualified to hold high office. I understood that she placated the reactionary Tea Party wing of the party and the gun loving Second Amendment fanatics, but why should the party of Lincoln cater to the fringe?

2012 was better. Mitt Romney, despite being a member of the Mormons, a religion that seems to defy reason (I mean who can really believe that Joseph Smith, in 1823 Western New York, found prophetic golden plates—the Book of Mormon—written in an unknown language which he translated into English with the help of *Moroni,* an angel who appeared only to him and who afterwards took the plates back to Heaven), was an outstanding candidate, morally upright, very intelligent and an experienced and capable politician. I didn't blame Mitt for following in the religion of his forefathers. And his running mate, Paul Ryan, was, I felt, an excellent choice for Vice President.

2016 was a different story. I think I might have met Donald Trump at my friend's bar mitzvah party in the 60's. Rollo was a terrible student in elementary school and his parents, who were quite well to do, sent him off to the New York Military Academy, a school with a reputation among my peers at the time for academic failures and those with severe disciplinary problems. Donald was in the class ahead of him. Rollo's bar mitzvah party was at Sherry's 1890, a fancy New York restaurant. His parents had booked the whole restaurant for the Saturday night after the bar mitzvah ceremony. They hired long white limousines to transport his friends from our Long Island suburb to the restaurant. After we were seated, a contingent from the military academy marched into the hall, resplendent in their fancy-dress uniforms and ceremonial swords. Rollo was among them. Although I'm not positive that Trump was there, he could have been.

I remembered Donald Trump from the early 80's when his main real estate company went bankrupt. He was personally liable for most of the debt. I was a bankruptcy attorney in Cleveland at the time and his was one of the largest Chapter 11's in New York. I marveled at his ability to convince his creditors to let him keep his yacht and receive a salary of $400,000 a month to try to reorganize his company. And this was when $400,000 a month was *real money*. Of course, I was more in awe of his attorneys' abilities to secure that kind of deal for him, but, still, he was an impressive self-promoting salesman. Since the early 80's he had gone on to ruin numerous other businesses, including casinos, golf courses and the massively fraudulent Trump University. The real estate business in New York is one of the dirtiest businesses in the city. I had known a lawyer whose whole practice was to go before the city's real estate tax board to reduce the evaluation of his client's properties. There's nothing illegal about this, but there is something unsavory about it. When applying for bank loans the common practice is to inflate the value of the properties and when applying for a reduction in real estate tax the practice is to minimize their value.

Trump regularly stiffed his attorneys, agents,

subcontractors and his employees. Not that this is uncommon in that industry, but he was famous for ripping people off. His reputation, even among the crowd of sharp and shady Manhattan real estate investors and developers, was particularly unsavory. After several of his business failures, New York banks avoided him, and he was only able to get loans from foreign banks, like Deutsche Bank, which ended up losing hundreds of millions of dollars in loan money to him. His reality TV show, "The Apprentice", rescued him from another crushing bankruptcy and gave him oodles of money for other ventures. It's curious, that a guy with no aptitude for running a business and the opposite of a Midas touch (he lost almost all the hundreds of millions he inherited from his father), but with an outsized ego, successfully played a fantasized version of himself. And what can be seen to be a takeoff from Gilbert and Sullivan's *The Mikado*—"He played his role so perfectly that now he is the ruler of the whole country."

He was a serial adulterer. He's been married and divorced several times. He's paid off porn stars and Playmates not to divulge sordid details of his relationships with them (although that didn't work out too well for him). He's been charged with rape numerous times and of course, there was that scandalous Access Hollywood tape before his election in 2016, boasting of his predatory behavior and his contempt for women. I couldn't understand why any normal Republican would want this guy for their presidential nominee. He was the opposite of what I thought the party stood for—probity, intelligence, thoughtfulness, politeness, and solid moral ethics. But he did have some powerful supporters.

Aside from his "base," which includes white supremacists, anti-Semites, assault rifle-toting right-wing militia types, he also had the overwhelming support of evangelical Christians. That was more puzzling. One would think that they would favor someone who was a paragon of Christian values—which includes fidelity to one's spouse, humility, clean speech, love and charity for the poor, etc. Trump had none of these qualities. But he did espouse the sacredness of the Second Amendment a desire to overturn the decision in *Roe*, a respect for the Confederacy and implied white supremacy, a hatred for the "Deep State" which evangelicals have told me is a code phrase for Jews, and building the Wall to keep out all those huddled poor and starving Christian masses who were escaping death, extreme violence, and poverty in lawless South and Central America. For all their supposed "religious" values, the Evangelicals were more interested in the "gun culture" and overturning *Roe v. Wade*. That was puzzling but not surprising. What really surprised me was the support he had among my own community, the Orthodox Jewish community of America.

The unifying factor in their support was not any value they saw in Trump as a person, but in terms of his ability to give us what we wanted. In fact, most Orthodox Jews viewed him as a flawed individual, but one we could work with. Sorry to say that in the opinion of many, his language and behavior was typical of *goyim*. Trump may be more open and less ashamed of his misogynistic, racist, and deplorable speech and behavior. But, at least, he didn't hide it, as most "respectable" *goyim* do. He was no more flawed than any other politician—like Roosevelt, Kennedy, and Clinton—all Democrats. He was just unashamed and therefore more honest. This is a very cynical way to look at American Democracy. What can I get out of this candidate? Not that there is necessarily something wrong in supporting a candidate who you hope will do things that will please you. In fact, that really is the essence of politics. However, when that candidate is anti-democratic, supported by unapologetic anti-Semites and a quasi-fascist, one would think that Jews would think twice about supporting him.

By the end of his term of office, these Jews had good reason to justify their support. Trump opened the U.S. Embassy in Jerusalem and by doing so proved to the world that contrary to Obama's Secretary of State, John Kerry's predictions of a pan Arab revolt following the removal of the Embassy to Jerusalem, nothing happened. Trump also recognized Israel's claims to the Golan Heights. Jewish development in East Jerusalem and Gush Etzion has been booming since Trump took office, in contrast to the freeze imposed upon us by the Obama Administration. No Arab country started a war with Israel over these moves and even the Palestinian reaction was much more subdued than expected. In fact, the opposite happened. Arab states have slowly been giving diplomatic recognition to Israel. Our relations with our Arab neighbors had never been better. We still have as enemies, Iran, and its proxies, like Hezbollah in Lebanon and Assad in Syria and Hamas in Gaza, who are planning for our annihilation but, in addition to Egypt, Jordan and Turkey, we now have full diplomatic relations with The United Arab Emirates, Morocco and Sudan, with, hopefully, more to come. In addition, by pulling out of the Joint Comprehensive Plan of Action with Iran, labeling Iran as a state sponsor of terrorism, and eliminating the vastly talented head of the Iranian Revolutionary Guard, Qaseem Soleimani, Israel and American Jews were very pleased with Trump's foreign policy in the Middle East.

In additional nods to the Orthodox community in America, Trump also pardoned Rabbi Rubashkin, the owner of a major kosher meat processing plant in Iowa who many felt was wrongly convicted of financial fraud and who received a disproportionately long sentence. He also pardoned Jonathan Pollard, a U.S. intelligence analyst who gave information to Israel about Arab military movements that the US, while obligated to turn over, was hiding from the Israelis. Although he pled guilty to the charge of espionage, Pollard was sentenced to life imprisonment—even after a plea deal was reached, because of a highly prejudiced Jewish apostate, U.S. Secretary of Defense, Casper Weinberger, who intervened with the judge, demanding that Pollard spend his life in prison, a sentence that no American spy for Russia in peacetime had ever received.

In addition, the nomination and confirmation of conservative federal judges and Supreme Court Justices, was something that Orthodox Jews supported. For all the above I must give the "devil his due" and thank Trump.

But aside from these positive things, Trump was a disaster as a president. As John Bolton writes in his book "The Room Where It Happened", Trump was noted for his abysmal disinterest in governing. He wanted to have the title of President with all the prerequisites of the office, but without any of the "boring" duties. He had no patience (or ability) for reading the briefing books given to him to read each day. Even the one-page summaries that every department briefing him had to provide were too much for him. (I can imagine that his presidential library will probably consist of video reruns of "The Apprentice," Fox and Friends, and Tucker Carlson, Donald's own ghost-written book "The Art of the Deal", and comic books). He didn't even have the interest to listen to those briefing him on vital matters of state. He watched TV throughout his briefings and for many hours a day while munching on Big Macs and KFC. The rest of his time he spent golfing or Tweeting insults about all his supposed enemies.

As did his niece, Dr. Mary Trump, I'm sure that other psychologists and psychiatrists will have a field day in the future writing about his damaged and warped relationship with his cruel and overbearing father and his psychotic mother. And no doubt, he was deeply damaged by his upbringing. But he is responsible for his behavior and after being nominated a second time for president by the Republicans I would have expected a different reaction to him than four years earlier.

But I was surprised. His support only seemed to increase. Or, at least, more people voted for him in 2020 than they did in 2016. Unfortunately for him, more people voted for Biden, not only in the total voting population of the United States where Biden had a margin of over 7 million votes, but also in those states needed to win election in the Electoral College—which, by the way, is the most idiotic and undemocratic way to select a president in the modern world.

As far as I know, there is no other democratic country that has such an unrepresentative process for choosing the national leader as the Electoral College. But, as ridiculous as it might be, it's never been changed. Why shouldn't there be a direct election for president? And why shouldn't the ballot for president be the same in every state? Why are voting procedures in each state different? What are Americans afraid of? I understand that at the beginning of the country, a deal had to be worked out between the separate colonies to come together and create a national government. Southern agricultural States with small populations of whites but with large numbers of non-voting slaves, wanted to have a louder voice in Congress than they would have been entitled to if only the total number of white voters nationwide were counted. They were allowed to count each slave in their state as ⅔ of a man for purposes of assessing the number of Congressmen their State would receive in the House of Representatives and in the Electoral College. I understand why the defeated Southern States after the Civil War wanted to eliminate the Black voter from the ballot box but keep their number of electoral votes. But in 21st Century America, it's the height of hypocrisy for a country, which promotes itself as the paragon of Democracy, to not elect its president by a majority vote of the voters. It means that if I live in New York or California, liberal states, my vote for the Republican Presidential candidate is worthless. I might as well stay home.

By the summer of 2020, polls showed that Trump had little chance of winning the election against Biden and the numbers didn't change up to Election Day. To prepare his supporters for the possibility of that loss he cranked up the "Stop the Steal" campaign. The NY Times traced the origin of the "Stop the Steal" campaign back to the self-proclaimed "dirty trickster" Roger Stone and the 2016 election. Since Trump and Stone assumed that Trump would lose that election, he wanted an excuse so that he could announce that he really won but "crooked Hillary" and the Democrats stole the election from him. To his surprise he won. Not one to waste a perfectly good smear campaign, his victory didn't stop Trump from maintaining that he really won the popular vote too, but Hillary's three million vote margin was a result of either illegally cast votes by non-citizens or Democrat manufactured and fraudulent ballots. His motivation in broadcasting the Big Lie was obvious. He, to whom the name "loser" is like kryptonite to Superman, could not bear to face the truth of a loss. In the run up to the 2020 election, he sent up a constant barrage of Tweets predicting that he would win the election unless he was cheated out of it by the Democratic thieves who would rig the election or stuff the ballot boxes with fake votes or manage, with help from the Chinese, to hack into the voting machines and change the votes from Trump to Biden; or that Hugo Chavez, the dead dictator of Venezuela would somehow get his revenge on Trump from beyond the grave with software for voting machines that he or his cronies somehow "fixed" with the support of George Soros, the Jewish devil, who owned the company that manufactured the voting machines (absolutely false). He has never conceded defeat and in countless Tweets and speeches, screamed that he had actually won the election by a landslide, but the Democrats somehow had changed the votes. Even in those states, like Georgia, where all the state election officials, including the governor were staunch Trump supporting Republicans, they had somehow been bribed to say that Biden won.

The very surprising thing was not that Trump could spout lies or conspiracies or retweet conspiracy theories from Alex Jones or QAnon—he has been a leading conspiracy theory proponent for years. It's not even surprising that according to the Republican Senate Majority Leader, Mitch McConnell, Trump was responsible for the failed insurrection at the Capitol Building on January 6th, against the Legislative Branch of the Government, which was in the process of ratifying the 2020 election results. Or that also according to McConnell he so abdicated his responsibilities as president and was so immoral that he was willing to end our democracy and see the country come to a flaming end. The astonishing thing is that according to poll after poll to date, between 70–80% of Republican Voters or 50 million Americans believed Trump that he won by a landslide, but the election was stolen from him.

What that means is that 50 million Americans are ready to believe a "Big Lie" from an election-losing sociopathic demagogue with fascist tendencies and to be ruled by him by fiat – regardless of the true election results.

As Bolton notes, Trump was very uninterested in the mechanics of the executive office he held. His attention span was infinitesimal and basically all he wanted to talk about with his cabinet members and his staff was himself. Imagine if a charismatic leader arises who is calculating, shrewd, and intimately familiar with the workings of government. And imagine that this person also has charisma and a talent for using the media. He would have at least fifty million Americans who would be interested in changing the American democratic government to a dictatorship that spouted Trump-like "values" of anti-immigration, white supremacy, physical violence toward those on the Left, hostility to the "Deep State", lower taxes for the rich, suppressing votes of those who don't share those same values, and as the Proud Boys expressed in the lead up to the January 6th insurrection: "Hail to the Emperor Trump."

The most troubling aspect of all this is that among those Trump supporters and believers in his Big Lies are many very intelligent people. I have been struggling to find an explanation as to why so many of my friends believe him. When asked what the evidence is, they reply with stories they've read on various right-wing websites pointing out "glitches" in machines or voting by dogs or dead grandparents or Republicans who couldn't get into the polling places to watch the count, or to mail-in ballots that were falsified by the Democrats.

Trump tried to have the election upset by the Judiciary. He

brought over sixty lawsuits and had lost virtually everyone because of insufficiency or lack of evidence. And of course, these weren't only Democratically appointed judges, but many were ones that he himself appointed—even the overwhelmingly conservative U.S. Supreme Court refused to hear his baseless claims. So how do my friends answer that seemingly insurmountable argument against their theory? They say that the courts were afraid to upset the vote because they were worried about the stability of the country. But, of course, that's not a legal argument, it's just a convenient explanation so that they can continue believing Trump's Big Lie.

Recently, Trump has been found liable in a case brought in New York by the writer E. Jean Carroll for a sexual assault that took place in a Manhattan department store in the 1990s. She won a verdict of $5,000,000 and then, attacking her after the first verdict, she sued for defamation and won a further award of $83 million. He's been indicted by a New York prosecutor for criminal election fraud involving payoffs to a porn star. He's recently been criminally indicted in Federal Court in Florida on 37 counts of violations, mostly of the Espionage Act, related to the illegal taking, storage and handling of classified government documents, refusal to return them when requested by the Government, and obstruction of justice.

The indictment is so specific and damning that even Trump's former Attorney General, Bill Barr said that if even half of the charges are true "he's toast". Trump, unsurprisingly, pleaded "not guilty". His explanation for the charges is that the Democrats are out to get him and that this and other cases against him are the result of a witch hunt by the "weaponized" Biden Justice Department. The irony is that Trump ran against Hillary Clinton in 2016 with the slogan: "Lock her up" for her alleged unsecured handling of her personal email account while Secretary of State. Now they're coming to "Lock him up." And, of course, there's more. Fulton County Georgia's prosecutor charged Trump and 18 other co-conspirators with trying to alter the results of the Georgia presidential election in 2020 One damning piece of evidence was Trump's call to Brad Raffensperger, the Republican Georgia Attorney General, asking him to find just over 11,000Trump votes so that he could overturn his loss in that state. Unfortunately for Trump, Raffensperger recorded the call. And then there are all the indictments involving the January 6, 2021, insurrection at the Capitol, where Trump tried to hold onto power by disrupting Congress' certification of the results of 2020 president election.

Insanely enough, Trump's popularity with Republicans has only increased with the cascade of his legal troubles. He is, by far, the leading contender for the Republican nomination for President in 2024.

Republican politicians, including his primary rivals, are understandably afraid of Trump. He is vengeful toward anyone whom he perceives as being even slightly disloyal. And even out of the White House he carries major clout in the party. Only a few of the most courageous Republican politicians had voted to impeach him or found him guilty of the impeachment charges or criticized him for his refusal to concede the election or to even condemn him for violations of handling of classified and sensitive material and obstruction of justice.

What is the psychology of those 50 million Trump voters who support the conspiracy theories of the "stolen election," which includes approximately 10-17 million QAnon followers? An excellent article in the New York Times of February 3, 2021, by Thomas B. Edsell, lays it out. In it he references research done by two academics Joseph E. Uscinski and Adam M. Enders, professors of political science at the University of Miami and the University of Louisville, who explore what they identify as some of the characteristics of the subscribers to the QAnon movement.

These include antisocial personality traits and a predisposition toward conspiracy thinking, rather than traditional political identities and motivations. Their adherents are not necessarily ideologically extreme – just extreme and antisocial.

But, what about my friends who are not otherwise extreme or antisocial or don't have a predisposition toward nonnormative behavior?

There is another explanation. In an interview of Professor Jovan Byford by Ian Florance for the September 2021 issue of *Psychologist*, a publication of the British Psychological Society, the author quotes a paragraph from Byford's 2011 book, *Conspiracy Theories: A Critical Introduction:*

"The defining feature of paranoia is the immediacy of threat and its personal nature: paranoid people see themselves as being under imminent personal threat. In conspiracy theories the threat is to a nation, religion, way of life, or the whole world, and it is seen as a part of a sinister long-term plan. Rather than looking for similarities between conspiracy beliefs and symptoms of psychiatric disorders, we need to turn our attention to the often unacknowledged benefits that belief in conspiracy theories brings to the believer, including the "illusion of control" and a sense that the world is ordered. But the most important benefit is the belief that one is part of some heroic minority that actually knows what is going on. That's a huge generator of self-esteem and what drives people to conspiracy theories."

There is much to recommend this opinion. Most of the Trump believers I know (I distinguish between believers—those who believe whatever he says, and supporters—who agree with his policies but don't necessarily accept his pronouncements as the truth) are not crackpots or paranoiacs who believe that the world is out to get them. They might be, like Trump, sore losers, but, then again, I'm sure that at least an equal number of Democrats are also sore losers. On the other hand, as to being part of a "heroic minority that actually knows what's going on", doesn't the losing side in an election always feel that they are the "heroic minority" and that the winners don't know what's really going on? They don't have to believe in conspiracy theories to think of themselves as such. And if those who subscribe to conspiracy theories derive feelings of self-esteem from being part of the "heroic minority" in the know, it means that they were somewhat lacking in self-esteem before they joined the "heroic minority" in the know. In which case, while not necessarily suffering from paranoia, they are suffering from some other personality defect. Therefore, a psychological explanation is not uncalled for.

Trump legitimized a yearning, in the hearts of many of our countrymen, to return to the days before racial, gender and political correctness—a world in which, they can say, as Trump does, whatever they want to say without a thought to its effect. They envy Trump for his "frank speech," like denigrating women and say openly that they're objects of his lascivious desires and he can act on those desires, even by forcing himself on them, because he knows "they really want it". And if the president says it's okay to think and talk like that, well then, who's to argue?

The same is true with race. In the old days, one could have a Black friend at school or work and truly not consider oneself a racist and yet harbor negative and demeaning views of most Blacks—the ones we didn't know. Our Black friends were exceptions and that could lend to an explanation of Obama's victory. He was supported by many whites who later voted for Trump. He was very intelligent and articulate and spoke like a white man. After all, his mother was white. One could vote for him hoping for a change in the economic recession of 2008 and feel good that by doing so you weren't a racist. Trump, by his coded messages about race, legitimizes his supporters' feelings about race and still feels that "he's the least racist person in the room" – even if that room is filled with Black people.

But, when all is said and done, we Jews firmly believe that *Hashem* runs the world. He is the one who determines who will be the leaders of government and what the shape of history will take. Although at first glance this might seem to be a contradiction. How can *Hashem* determine history and still allow individuals to have free will? Our Sages have taught us how to resolve this conundrum.

As it says in *Bereshis*:

"As the sun was about to set, a deep sleep fell upon Abram, and a great dark dread descended upon him. And He [God] said to Abram, Know well that your offspring shall be strangers in a land not their own, and they shall be enslaved and oppressed for four hundred years; but I will execute judgment on the nation they shall serve, and in the end, they shall go free with great wealth...And they shall return here in the fourth generation, for the sins of the Amorites are not yet complete" *(Bereshit* 15:12–14,16).

Abram was not told that his offspring would be slaves in

Egypt, only that their slavery and oppression would be in a "land not theirs."

While the general history of the children of Abraham was set by G-d, the specifics were not. Our Sages say that Pharaoh and the Egyptians took that task upon themselves. Another nation could have been the one to enslave Abraham's offspring. Likewise, what "slavery" and "oppression" to be suffered was also undefined. Pharaoh could have enslaved the Jewish people for one day, instead of over eighty years. He didn't have to be so cruel in his treatment of his slaves—he didn't have to kill the baby boys. All that was a result of Pharaoh's free will. The first seven plagues were the result of Pharaoh's freely made decision to disregard G-d's warnings, only for the last three did *Hashem* harden Pharaoh's heart so that, according to some commentators, he lacked free will.

Likewise, when the Jews in the desert worshiped the Golden Calf, that was wholly by free will, not by Divine decree. Otherwise, how could the Nation be punished for something that was beyond their control?

Whenever prophets prophesy that in a given number of years something will happen, we don't know how to count those years. So, while the prophecy to Abram was that the Jews would be strangers and slaves in a strange land for 400 years, in retrospect, the Sages say, the count actually began with the birth of Yitzchok. The actual amount of time that Jews were in Egypt was only 210 years and in only 80 of those years was our Nation enslaved and oppressed in the manner that we read about in the *Haggadah*. The other 190 years were also called "slavery", but it was perhaps slavery to other ideologies or to our own unholy thoughts. So "slavery" doesn't have to mean suffering under the whip or being thrown into jail. One can be a slave to one's desires and oppressed by one's thoughts. *Hashem* sketches out the big picture, but Man fills in the blanks.

A friend of mine, Rabbi Noam Lesser, recently wrote a very interesting piece about the slavery of the Jews in Egypt. Because the Jewish people needed to become slaves to *Hashem*, slavery to another nation was a prerequisite to prepare them for that mission. We were free people before our exile in Egypt. And even though our forefathers and their families were righteous and served *Hashem* with great devotion, they did so because they wanted to, and not because they were obligated to. They acted as individuals, but *Hashem* wanted us to serve Him as a nation. We needed to experience slavery as a nation so that we could understand what it meant when *Hashem* commanded our nation to accept the Torah and to become obligated to him and to his *mitzvohs*. And after we understood what it meant to be a slave to *Hashem* and to serve Him out of obligation and fear, only then could we rise to the higher level and serve Him also out of love.

This idea that *Hashem* runs the world and directs the course of history brings me back to politics. As I heard in the name of a well-known *Rosh HaYeshiva* when speaking about Trump's election in 2016: "I knew when Trump won the Republican nomination for President in 2015 after defeating a field of nineteen **normal** politicians, that he would win the Presidency. It's impossible that such a lying, boastful, crazy, low life could have become the Republican nominee, unless *Hashem* willed it so." Whatever his faults, Israel benefited from him. So, we have to be thankful for the good that Trump brought and thankful that he's gone, at least for the moment. As the leading candidate for the Republican nomination for President in the 2024 election, the saga continues.

CHAPTER XXVI
Reflection on Life in Jerusalem

I have been very fortunate and blessed to live for the last thirty-five years in Jerusalem. Although I have traveled a great deal for work since I moved here, I much prefer to stay home. Of course, with a brother and sister, children and grandchildren in New York, the unpleasantness of travel to America is somewhat mitigated. But I would prefer to stay where I am and that they come to me.

What is it that I love about Jerusalem? I say Jerusalem and not Israel, because to me, while all Israel is holy and beautiful, I feel Jerusalem's holiness and beauty more palpably. It's hard to describe exactly what I mean, since it's a feeling and not a logical thought. There is a famous *Gemara Kiddushin* 49b that says:

"Ten parts of beauty were given to the world and Jerusalem received nine parts."

And another in the *Gemara Kesuvos* 110b:

"If a wife wants to move to Jerusalem from any part of Israel, the husband can be forced to comply with her wishes."

Why is that? Because it's the holiest place in Israel, which is the holiest land in the world.

Rabbi Meir says, "Whoever has established permanent residence in the Land of Israel, speaks *lashon hakodesh* (Hebrew, the holy language of the Torah), eats produce only after *terumah* and *ma'aser* (tithes) have been separated and recites the *Shema Yisrael* prayer in the morning and evening—can be assured of having a place in the World to Come."
Shekalim 9b

In other words, if a person lives in the place where *Hashem* wants him to live, speaks in the language that *Hashem* wants him to speak, eats what *Hashem* wants him to eat and has an ongoing prayer-communication connection to the One

Hashem—he is living in accordance with his Creator's Will and will certainly merit eternal life.

The place where the Holy of Holies stood, the most sacred space in the Temple and, therefore, the universe, atop the Temple Mount, is now covered by the Dome of the Rock, a Muslim monument. From that Rock, in a process that physicists have called the Big Bang Theory, *Hashem* created the universe. From the void, *Hashem* created an atom of matter, the tiniest particle, *ex nihilo*—from nothing, and from that particle he extruded the entire and expanding universe. That original matter, that seed of the universe, He placed here, in my city, on the Temple Mount, that rock upon which would be the place of the Binding of Isaac. I cannot visit the exact spot, because after the Six Day War, the Israelis gave supervising authority to the Jordanian *Waqf* (a Moslem religious foundation) as a peace gesture. In gratitude, the *Waqf* forbade Jews to trespass on that piece of Jerusalem. But since Jewish law forbids us to go there in our present state of impurity, which can only be rectified by the return of the *Moshiach*, it's just as well. In fact, it's for the best, since if we administered that area, we wouldn't be able to stop Jews from going there.

But I can go near it. I can stand at the Western Wall and pray and feel the emanations that are still reverberating from that Rock. In fact, I don't have to stand at the Western Wall to feel them. I can feel them in my home or my *shul* or my *Yeshiva* which are all about 1.5 kilometers away.

What is *Kedusha*—holiness? There is a legalistic definition and a poetic one—a spiritual definition. The word itself means separation or consecration. Jewish Marriage is called *"kiddushin"* implying that the union of the man and woman is consecrated for a unique and holy purpose. It can also indicate the opposite. A prostitute is called a *"kadeisha"*—someone separated for an immoral purpose.

In Temple times it referred to a physical object or physical place that was consecrated to the Almighty, rendering it the property of the Temple, or to its custodians, or to a beneficiary of holy things, such as a *Cohen* or a *Levi*. Once consecrated, it does not belong to me anymore. I might have an obligation to care for it until I deliver it to the Temple or to the *Cohen* or *Levi*, but it's not my property.

Let's say I have unintentionally committed a sin. For example, I unwittingly carried a cellphone in a public place on the Sabbath, thinking that it was Thursday. I am required to bring a sin offering to the Temple. I purchase a sheep and designate it for my sacrifice. It now has *Kedusha*. It no longer belongs to me, but to G-d. On my next trip to the Temple, I'll bring it along and sacrifice it. Or let's say I have a desire to make a gift of my camel (an animal that is forbidden to brought as a sacrifice) to the Temple for them to use as they see fit. I can be *makdish* it—consecrate it and give it to the Temple treasurer and he can sell it or use it as he sees fit.

But today there is no Temple and the Torah's legalistic definition hardly applies anymore, but for one major exception—the Land of Israel itself.

When the Jewish Nation first came into the Land, after traveling from Egypt through the desert for forty years, we conquered the Canaanite inhabitants and consecrated the Land making it literally—The Holy Land. Because the Land belongs to G-d who gave it to the Jewish People as its custodians, there are many rules that apply to it. We are not free to use it in any way we please.

To my knowledge the Jews are the only People in the World who have the concept of *Yovel*—The Jubilee Year. Every fifty years, while the Temple was in existence, the Land reverted to the original families to whom it was allocated after the original conquest. Even though I might have sold my farm during the previous fifty years, it comes back to me at no cost. In effect, my sale is really a fifty-year lease and I have a right of redemption during that time if my fortunes turn. This is based on the idea that no one would ever willingly sell his ancestral land.

There are also Sabbatical years, every seventh year. These are still observed in Israel, although on a rabbinic level. At the end of that year all debts are forgiven and during it we are not allowed to work the Land, export its produce to a foreign country, or to sell its produce. The fruits of the Land are free to anyone who wants to come to my farm and harvest them. There are also gifts that must be given to the *Cohen* and *Levi* and the poor, from every harvest. Those laws are also kept today on a rabbinic level. And there are other laws and *mitzvohs* that pertain to the Land because of its holiness.

Is there another place like this in the World? If there is, I never heard of it. We literally see in practice that this is *Hashem's* Land and can extrapolate from it a recognition that the whole World belongs to Him. We are not owners, only tenants, living from His magnificence. What a privilege it is to be able to live here and experience *Hashem's* sovereignty every day.

In short, *Kedusha* still exists today.

But that is not the *Kedusha* that I feel in Jerusalem. It may contribute to it—knowing that I live in a Land that has these rules, which even though I'm not a farmer, still involves me because I consume the fruits and vegetables which are produced here, and have an obligation to make sure that such produce has been properly tithed, etc.

What I'm talking about is something much more esoteric. It's a feeling, perhaps aided also by the knowledge that my ancestors *davened* three times a day for thousands of years yearning to be able to come here, to G-d's Land.

The first time I experienced that feeling was in the summer of 1968. I was between my junior and senior years of college and with two of my friends I spent the summer traveling around Europe and Israel. We had flown to London and after spending a week there took the ferry to Calais where we rented a boxy Citroen and drove through France and Italy. We left our car in Venice and took a train through the Balkans to Greece. From Athens we flew to Tel Aviv. As we walked from our *pension* to the beach, the first thing that struck me was that everyone was Jewish—even the policemen and garbage men. It was an extraordinary feeling. Coming from New York, where there were plenty of Jews, but many more *goyim,* and rare was the policeman and the garbage man who was Jewish, to come to a country where almost everyone was Jewish and did all the things that *goyim* did at home was both discordant and very heartwarming.

When we got to Jerusalem, we stayed in Arab East Jerusalem—literally a stone's throw from where we live today. The reason was that the week before we arrived there were a spate of bombings by Arabs in the Jewish part of the city and I felt we'd be safer with the Arabs, who wouldn't openly attack us in their area.

This was a year after the Six Day War, when the Arabs were subdued. We Jews were filled with pride at our amazing achievements. We were feeling on top of the world, and as hard as it is to believe today, the world was on our side. Nasser had gambled and lost. He thought that with his alliance with Syria, creating the United Arab Republic and with support from Jordan and the rest of the Arab World he could finally "throw the Jews into the sea" as he had threatened many times before to do. When he cut our access to the Red Sea by blocking the Straits of Tiran, it was an act of war. And Nasser was seen by the nations of the world for what he was—a dangerous bully, who wanted to exterminate the remainder of the Jewish Nation that Hitler had failed to kill. Hardly any nation sees Israel in that light today. Now we're the ones that have earned the opprobrium of the world for just trying to stay alive.

So, there we were in Jerusalem, Victor, Tovar and me, a year after that great victory. The Western Wall, which the Jordanians had refused to give us access to, from the War of Independence in 1948 to 1967, was now ours. The dense Arab housing that was in its vicinity had been cleared away. The area in front of the wall was unpaved, but it was more "authentic" than today's beautifully paved plaza.

The morning after we arrived in Jerusalem we walked

down to the Wall—about twenty minutes from our *pension*. I was immediately accosted by a 13-year-old Lubovitch kid who asked me if I had put on tefillin that morning. I answered, "no, I haven't put on tefillin since the day after my bar mitzvah." He wrapped me in tefillin and asked me to repeat the prayers after him. As I did, I sobbed uncontrollably – in part because I felt the *Kedusha* of this holy place, and in part because I was now standing in the place where my ancestors stood 2000 years ago and was wrapped in tefillin as they were. If only Nani-Nani, my extremely pious great grandmother could see me now. She'd be so proud. But I was also crying because I was embarrassed that I needed a thirteen-year-old to help me to pronounce the *berachos*. I was ashamed that I was an irreligious ignoramus.

That moment changed me. I would never be the same person I was before. And even though I didn't become religious on the spot, when my life moved in that direction, I didn't fight it, but welcomed it. More than fifty years later, I still remember that day as one in which the *Kedusha* that was invested in a place well over 3000 years ago was still present and it changed me.

Jerusalem must have the clearest sky in the World. When it's not raining, and it doesn't rain from April to November, the sky is the most intense blue I have ever seen. On some days it's a deep sapphire blue. When it is, I can't stop looking at it. It's so beautiful. Other days it's just very blue and beautiful. Sometimes after a rain the sky is filled with clouds that look like angel wings. I've never seen a more beautiful sky.

It is fitting that the Torah says, "Speak to the Israelite people and instruct them to make *tzitzis* for themselves on the corners of their garments through all the ages; let them attach a cord of blue to the *tzitzis* of each corner. That shall be your *tzitzi*s; look at it and recall all of God's commandments and observe them... Thus, shall you be reminded to observe all My commandments and to be holy to your God. I the Lord am your God, who brought you out of the land of Egypt to be your God..."(Numbers 15: 38–41).

The Gemara *Menachos* quotes Rabbi Meir asking rhetorically about blue being used for the *tzitzit*. "Why is blue different from all other colors? Because blue resembles the sea, and the sea resembles sky, and the sky resembles God's Throne of Glory... as it is written: 'Above the sky over their heads was the semblance of a throne, like sapphire in appearance...'" *Menachos* 43b

So, when we look at the blue thread of the *tzitzit* we are reminded of *Hashem's* throne and of His Sovereignty. I don't have blue in my *tzitzis* (my *halachic* authorities say that we have lost the knowledge of which mollusk or fish produces the blue dye called *techelis*) but I can look at the sky in Jerusalem and be reminded of G-d's throne.

And the city is beautiful. The buildings are all faced with what's called "Jerusalem stone"—an off-white sandstone that is filled with crystal-like minerals that sparkle like diamonds in the sunlight. In the evening, when the sun goes down, the stones turn pink. And the walls of the Old City, built during the Ottoman period, are high, maybe sixty feet high and thick and beautiful. The *Gemara* isn't lying when it says that nine tenths of beauty in the world fell to Jerusalem. And I'm sure that its beauty is nothing compared to its beauty when the Temple was standing. As it says in the *Gemara:*

"He who has not seen Herod's building (the Temple), has never seen a beautiful building in his lifetime." *Baba Basra* 4a.

We pray for the restoration of our Temple and the reign of

the *Moshiach, bemharah b'yamainu* (speedily in our days).

The End